THE PRACTICE OF FINDING

Warmly,

Holly

The
Practice
of
Finding

How Gratitude
Leads the Way to Enough

Holly W. Whitcomb

WILLIAM B. EERDMANS PUBLISHING COMPANY
GRAND RAPIDS, MICHIGAN

Wm. B. Eerdmans Publishing Co.
4035 Park East Court SE, Grand Rapids, Michigan 49546
www.eerdmans.com

25 24 23 22 21 20 19   1 2 3 4 5 6 7

ISBN 978-0-8028-7530-3

Library of Congress Cataloging-in-Publication Data

A catalog record for this book is available from the Library of Congress

Two poems by Wendell Berry—"The Wild Geese" on the opposite page
and "The Sycamore" on p. 53: Copyright © 1987 by Wendell Berry,
from *Collected Poems*. Reprinted by permission of Counterpoint Press.

The Wild Geese

Horseback on Sunday morning,
harvest over, we taste persimmon
and wild grape, sharp sweet
of summer's end. In time's maze
over the fall fields, we name names
that went west from here, names
that rest on graves. We open
a persimmon seed to find the tree
that stands in promise,
pale, in the seed's marrow.
Geese appear high over us,
pass, and the sky closes. Abandon,
as in love or sleep, holds
them to their way, clear,
in the ancient faith: what we need
is here. And we pray, not
for new earth or heaven, but to be
quiet in heart, and in eye
clear. What we need is here.

—Wendell Berry

Contents

Contents

Finding without Seeking

The path to heaven lies through heaven,
and all the way to heaven is heaven.

— Saint Catherine of Siena

Seek and ye shall find.

This single phrase joined together for all time two unrelated practices, two entirely different actions: seeking and finding. They are *not* the same thing. We can seek and seek and never find the one thing for which we have spent all our days upon the earth searching. On the other hand, on a particularly magical day, we may stumble upon something for which our heart has yearned for as many days as we can remember. And today, here it is! Right before us, on a day we were not even thinking of it at all.

In *The Practice of Finding*, Holly Whitcomb assures us that to be finders, we need not always be seekers. But we *must* be awake. Aware. Open, porous, taking in whatever is around us. Mindful of the world as it is.

For those of us trained in the art of hard work and improved results, the idea of finding without seeking may seem unfair. Those who have been striving, searching, seeking day after day without respite, surely *they* should get the reward. They are the ones who deserve to be finding. One cannot simply be a finder. That cannot be right. What of those who work hard to earn the blessings they seek—and deserve?

There is an important clue in the song "Amazing Grace," written by a repentant slave trader: grace cannot be earned but is always and only given. It is a gift bestowed by God, if and when God chooses. "'Twas grace that taught my heart to fear, and grace my fears relieved; / How precious did that grace appear the hour I first believed!"

Everything—the smell of cookies on a Ponderosa pine, the fragrance of earth after a thunderstorm, the color of the sunset, the feel of warm water in summer—is a gift. As both seekers and finders, we learn to take a more accurate inventory of this fullness that populates our life. We appreciate the whole truth of who we are, the complete richness of what we have, and the whole picture of what we have planted, grown, and harvested. Only then can we know we have taken a confident measure of the unimaginable totality of all we have received in this precious human life.

Unlike finding, seeking is always worried about the future. And our highest form of seeking is "progress." Progress is the road to a new, improved promised land. At the end of progress, we will all have peak efficiency, superior productivity, and an elevated standard of living. We will have thoroughly mastered nature and all its inherent problems, we will all live in a place and time in which all will be well, all diseases cured, all wars ended, and a chicken in every pot. We are on the glory road, we are hurtling toward the eschaton. There is no time to rest, because we are on a very important mission, to go boldly where no species has gone before. We never rest on our laurels, we never rest at all. Every moment is a necessary investment in the divinely ordained and completely unquestioned goal of progress. What we are building for the future is infinitely more important than whatever we have right now. The idea of progress is an inflated pyramid scheme, where our riches exist always to be mined and harvested in the future, through endlessly expanding markets; not here, not now but there and later we will see the promised land, we will make the big score, our ship will come in, we will get the pot of gold at the end of the rainbow, we will strike it rich, we will hit the jackpot, we will be on easy street.

If the promised land is the good and perfect place, then where we are right now must be an imperfect place, a defective place. If the future is sacred, then the present is imperfectly sinful. Every day we find we are still on the path to paradise, we begin another day of seeking, striving, working, another day in a long life of searching, each day a disappointment. The blessing of a human life, in spite of its miraculous beauty and wonder, is not—for the seeker—a breathtaking source of unfathomable grace.

But we must ask ourselves: What if we are not going anywhere? What if we are simply living and growing within an ever-deepening cycle of rhythms, perhaps getting wiser, perhaps learning to be kind, and hopefully passing to our children whatever we have learned? What if our life, rough-hewn from the stuff of creation, never ceases to create new beginnings? What if our life is simply a time we are blessed with both sadness and joy, health and disease, courage and fear—and all the while we work, pray, and love, knowing that the promised land we seek is already present in the very gift of life itself, the unbearable privilege of a human birth? What if this single human life is itself the jewel in the lotus, the treasure hidden in the field, the pearl of great price? What if all the way to heaven is heaven?

In *The Practice of Finding*, Holly Whitcomb asks us, with the deepest possible kindness and compassion, to consider this: What if we are now and always standing on sacred ground? What if the gifts of grace and delight are present and abundant; if the time to live and love and give thanks and rest and delight is now, this moment, this day? Feel what heaven is like; have a taste of eternity. Rest in the arms of the divine. Here, we are truly found.

We do not have miles to go before we sleep. The time to sleep, to rest, to take our pleasure, is now. Look around. We are already home.

WAYNE MULLER
Santa Fe
October 2018

The Practice of Finding:
How Gratitude Leads the Way to Enough

> When we are trapped in seeking, nothing is
> enough. Everything we have mocks us; we see
> only what is missing, and all that is already here
> seems pale and unsatisfying. . . . The time for
> seeking is over; the time for finding has begun.
>
> —Wayne Muller, *Sabbath*

To be a seeker is usually considered a positive attribute. A good friend of mine was a member of a group
called "The Seekers" at her church. These were open-
minded, curious folks who invited thought-provoking
guest speakers and who were continually educating
themselves on significant issues. Yet persistent striving, even for something positive such as more enlight-
enment, can become harmful. Seeking possesses the
potential to become obsessive and addictive if we're
insatiable and grasping. Will we ever be satisfied?
What is enough?

Perhaps what is enough is the antidote to chronic seeking: the spiritual practice of finding.

Practice finding. Practice finding. I've been saying that to myself a lot lately to become aware of my abundance and to counteract the message of scarcity and insufficiency that our commercial culture constantly pumps into us. The practice of finding is a doorway to gratitude and to the awareness of having received enough.

Author and Episcopal priest Barbara Brown Taylor says, "Many years ago now, when I was invited to speak at a church gathering, my host said, 'Tell us what is saving your life right now.'"[1] My answer to this pivotal question, then and now, is that the practice of finding has been saving my life for a long time. This practice is a faithful old friend that has stayed by my side during times of lavish joy and exuberance as well as times of debilitating grief and loss. The practice of finding has nudged me to consider important and illuminating questions:

> What has surprised you here?
> What have you discovered that
> you did not anticipate?

I depend on this discipline to help me take little for granted and to daily celebrate what is. The practice of finding helps me absorb the sweetness of an unexpected compliment and breathe in the fresh green smell of newly picked corn. The practice of finding reminds me to look for moments of grace and to savor the gifts of God's creation. It opens my heart to receive more deeply.

Here in Wisconsin, my husband, John, and I are members of a hiking club; we've trekked thousands of miles with companions on the trail. Besides being wonderful exercise, walking slows everything down. When we walk, our senses become finely honed, and we notice wonders large and small: mushrooms and wildflowers, ice floes and flood waters, spawning salmon and baby swans, Venus in the west and a harvest moon. When we explore the world on foot, new discoveries lie around every corner. When we're immersed in the rhythms of walking, we embody the practice of finding.

My early practices in finding were shaped by parents who were spontaneously grateful. Every day my father observed and commented on the glories of nature as he took in the shapes of clouds, the texture of grasses, the flight patterns of birds. I can still picture him slurping the autumn sweetness of a Golden Delicious apple, juice running down his chin and onto the ground. And because my parents were avid hikers, backpackers, cyclists, and canoeists, they trained my sister and me to notice and identify birds and animals, trees and rocks—the indigo bunting, the scarlet tanager, the bur oak—taking joy in nature's simple bounties.

In my mother's final weeks, she again became my teacher. Her practice of finding became most evident as she was dying. With a quiet humility she realized the shortness of her remaining time and her utter dependence on those around her. And in the midst of this profound sorrow, this terrible letting go, she taught me gratitude. In our visits during her last days, we witnessed her life change tenor. No longer did she strive. She was simply being. In those radiant, early summer days, I'd take her out in her wheelchair to the back parking lot of the hospice unit and then sit beside her on the curb. There we found a little sanctuary of woods and wildflowers. "Aren't the pine trees gorgeous?" she'd say.

"Yes. Can you smell them?" I'd respond. Back and forth we went, detailing our little sanctuary: "Isn't the sky blue and clear?" "Yes, not a cloud." Once we had the good fortune to see a deer browsing in the woods, and we talked about that for several days. My mother savored everything in her practice of finding.

As my own practice of finding deepened, I learned the gifts that even suffering can bring. Insights ripened through grief and disappointment taught me to view situations from many vantage points. I discovered that a good many of us are suffering at any given time, but in vastly different ways. Through those gained insights, I developed a strength and a sensitivity I hadn't experienced before.

As you read this book, my hope is that it will help you live into the fullness and plenitude that surround us. In the pages that follow, I reflect on wisdom distilled by the *finders:* poets, playwrights, psychologists, and theologians. As a fellow finder, I also share my own experiences. The practice of finding often takes our breath away and brings tears to our eyes, for through these precious and unforeseen "aha" moments we discover that the gift we receive is more cherished than the one we've been seeking.

When we engage in finding, we recognize in a kind of humility and wonder that the universe contains possibilities beyond our power to imagine. *The Practice of Finding* is a guide to that journey of discovery, which can prompt you to discern the gifts of both joy and suffering. In this book we'll explore together the particular gifts of savoring, blessing, saying yes, owning yourself, welcoming the Spirit, and waking up to what you already have and are.

Yes, you'll find some conventional and familiar "gratitudes" (as I like to call them) in this book, but you'll also discover surprising and unexpected ones. And as you come to the book's end, your practice of finding will be deepened and refined. Perhaps, like me, you'll marvel at what you already possess.

CHAPTER ONE

Learning to Savor and Finding Wonder

Most of our lives are busy and demanding, filled with the responsibilities of work or caregiving or both. In our frantic pace, we rarely pause to pay attention. We lose perspective because we're moving so fast. Yet when we do pause, everything changes: we listen to the morning quiet and take notice of the nuthatch or the sunlight filtering through the leaves of the Japanese maple. When we notice something lovely, the tenor of the whole day is changed, transformed from routine and obligation to revelation and delight. We become enchanted by small things. We become those who savor.

Although I have been a good savorer all my life, thanks to my dad's grateful heart and spontaneous jubilation, I didn't realize until recently how essential the work of savoring actually could be. In a special issue of *Time* magazine called "The Science of Happiness," an eminent researcher considers savoring a pivotal hallmark of leading a happy life.[1] Learning to savor is also a vital spiritual practice. An often repeated Jewish saying reminds us of this truth: "On the Day of Judgment God will only ask one question: Did you enjoy my world?"[2] When we savor—when we enjoy God's world—we live richer, deeper, more expansive lives. How can we learn to savor? Here are some simple suggestions.

Slow down and pay attention

Another lesson I learned from my father was to slow down. While he was spending time with me, he never talked on the phone, or read a magazine, or looked bored. He offered me his full attention as he waited eagerly for my story to unfold. Children adored him. If a small child talked to him while crawling on the floor, my dad would engage that child by getting down and crawling on the floor too. He was never too rushed to be aware. On the day and hour he died in 1998, my dad was out in the backyard, sitting in his wooden swing and feeding corn to the squirrels. At the moment of his death, he was relishing—savoring—the beauty of an April day.

In the last act of Thornton Wilder's beloved play *Our Town*, deceased Emily is allowed to come back to earth on a day of her choosing, and she picks her twelfth birthday. As the day ends, she says:

I didn't realize. So all that was going on and we never noticed. Take me back—up the hill—to my grave. But first: Wait! One more look.

Good-by, Good-by, world. Good-by, Grover's Corners. . . . Mama and Papa. Good-by to clocks ticking . . . and Mama's sunflowers. And food and coffee. And new-ironed dresses and hot baths . . . and sleeping and waking up. Oh, earth, you're too wonderful for anybody to realize you.

Do any human beings ever realize life while they live it—every, every minute?[3]

Simple pleasures shine when we slow down and pay attention. When I was seventeen, each of us who were seniors in my high school were given an entire page in the yearbook. I devoted my page to a large photo of myself carrying a backpack in front of a frozen waterfall with a quotation from Thoreau: "The man [or woman] is the richest whose pleasures are the cheapest."[4] Decades later, I still value simple pleasures. I'm overjoyed by a home-baked blueberry pie in summer or a walk on a spring evening or a candlelit hot bath in winter.

On November 21, 1793, Samuel Lane of Stratham, New Hampshire, a farmer, surveyor, shoemaker, and tanner, wrote in his diary, a journal he kept actively for sixty-five years. On this particular Thanksgiving

Day, he rose before daylight and recorded his "Many Mercies."

The Life & health of myself and family, and also of so many of my Children, grand Children & great grandchildren; also of my other Relations and friends & Neighbors, for Health peace and plenty amongst us.

for my Bible and Many other good and Useful Books, Civil & Religious Priviledges, for the ordinances of the gospel; and for my Minister.

for my Land, House and Barn and other Buildings, & that they are preserv'd from fire & other accidents.

for my wearing Clothes to keep me warm, my Bed & Beding to rest upon.

for my Cattle, Sheep & Swine & other Creatures, for my support.

for my Corn, Wheat, Rye Grass and Hay; Wool, flax, Syder, Apples, Pumpkins, Potatoes, Cabages, tirnips, Carrots, Beets, peaches and other fruits.

for my Clock and Watch to measure my passing time by Day and by Night,

Wood, Water, Butter, Cheese, Milk, Pork, Beefe, & fish, &c.

for Tea, Sugar, Rum, Wine, Gin, Molasses, peper, Spice & Money for to bye other Necessaries and to pay my Debts & Taxes, &c.

for my Lether, Lamp oyl & Candles, Husbandry Uten-
sils, & other tools of every sort &c &c &c.
Bless the Lord O my Soul and all that is within me
Bless his Holy Name. Bless the Lord O my Soul
and forget not all his benefits, who Satisfieth thy
mouth with good things &c.[5]

This reading, which I have shared with my family
at our Thanksgiving table, prompts us to make our
own lists of simple pleasures and gratitudes.

Dwell in the fullness of time

When we practice finding, we pay attention to time as
we consider the wondrous possibilities of the present,
the past, and the future.

Savoring the present means not being distracted
by the conundrums of the past or the worries of the
future, but remaining solidly in the here and now.
Buddhist monk and peace activist Thich Nhat Hanh
shares the Buddha's way of remaining present:

When the Buddha was asked, "Sir, what do you
and your monks practice?," he replied, "We sit, we
walk, we eat." The questioner continued, "But sir,
everyone sits, walks, and eats," and the Buddha told

him, "When we sit, we *know* we are sitting. When we walk, we *know* we are walking. When we eat, we *know* we are eating."[6]

The invitation to savor the past allows our good memories to comfort and sustain us. Good memories are stored-up treasure, keeping us going for a long, long time. Fourteen years ago, our congregation celebrated the twenty-fifth anniversary of my ordination. Church members made a big to-do over it, and I was thrilled with the whole thing. A few days after that celebration, I met with my spiritual director, explaining to her how much I cherished that deep and loving gift. Then I went right on to talk about something else. "Stop, Holly! Wait," she said. "Don't go on to another subject. Think about this beautiful celebration. Hold on to this precious memory and recount the details again in your heart. Let this memory sustain you as you ponder it again and again." I've never forgotten her words, and I now make a point of stopping to relive a good memory, holding it and savoring it, as the practice of finding reminds me to be nourished by past graces.

Learning to savor also allows us to welcome the future and appreciate anticipation.

Any of us who came of age in the seventies can easily sing along to Carly Simon's hit "Anticipation."

She wrote that entire song in fifteen minutes, when Cat Stevens (now Yusef Islam) was running late for their date.[7] Anticipation is precious. It exponentially increases our enjoyment of whatever good event we look forward to. Whenever I take an older person out for lunch or a ride or a walk, I try to call a couple of days ahead so they can savor the joyous anticipation of getting out of the house. Dr. Sonya Lyubomirsky, a prolific researcher on the science of happiness, reminds us that "the pleasure of the anticipation is valued almost as much as the experience being anticipated."[8] I have extensive training in anticipation because our children have lived in other countries: India, England, Switzerland. The necessity of buying our plane tickets months in advance has allowed my husband and me many weeks to savor the anticipation of being together once again. Living deeply into such anticipation helps us to enter fully into the prospect of delight that lies ahead.

Wake up to wonder

We cannot experience wonder if we think we've seen it all and know it all. Wonder requires a childlike openness and a beginner's mind. Anne Lamott comments incisively, "Wonder takes our breath away, and makes room for new breath. That's why they call it breathtaking."⁹ Wonder requires a certain emotional spaciousness and a keen attentiveness. In fact, if we don't stop and savor, wonder will pass us right by.

This past summer, my husband and I had the unique pleasure of observing the bat flight that occurs each night (from late April through October) at the original cave entrance of Carlsbad Caverns in New Mexico. On a June evening at dusk, we sat with eight hundred other people in a huge stone amphitheater waiting for the bats to emerge. As we chatted with new friends or e-mailed or looked at our Instagram feeds, the ranger announced that the bats could be leaving shortly. Because the bats' echolocation system is extremely sensitive, we couldn't put our cell phones on airplane mode, but needed to power them off completely. To encourage our cooperation and to ensure our silence, she mentioned that on a recent evening a man in the audience had sneezed during the bat flight, causing the bats to go berserk and to fly aimlessly in all directions. At 6:45 p.m. the ranger ceased her banter, put a finger to her lips, and said, "They're coming out now!" A grand hush fell over the crowd—and suddenly we sat in total silence except for the maniacal whirr of wings as bats rose in formation in an immense cylindrical column from the underground cave. Unexpectedly, I began to cry, not because I was frightened of the bats, but because I had never experienced such reverence over a natural phenomenon in a group so large. It was an awe-filled, holy moment of savoring God's creation. This giant, whirring column turned the sky black: 400,000 bats emerged in just half an hour, and the audience remained silent, mesmerized, transfixed.

Waking up to wonder means recognizing moments of reverence and transcendence of all kinds. Back in the 1990s, our family visited relatives in northern California and traveled to Kings Canyon and Sequoia National Parks. Now, I had seen pictures in books of giant sequoia trees, photos of the General Sherman tree, and even of the huge tree in Sequoia National Park that cars can drive right through. But no pictures prepared me adequately for the majesty and sheer sanctity of that giant tree called the sequoia.

The General Sherman tree, for example, has been on this earth during the Golden Age of Greece and the first Olympic games, the time of Alexander the Great and Julius Caesar, the birth and crucifixion of Jesus, the Mayan Indians' development of an advanced civilization in Central America and Mexico, the Tang Dynasty in China, Charlemagne, the Renaissance, the Reformation, and the birth of Protestantism. That is one ancient tree!

As I walked through the groves of sequoias in the park, I became aware that a certain decorum was in order. One did not run or scream or chase around these holy giants but instead chose to slow down and to savor. Incredulously, I passed bench after bench of tourists sitting in total silence, observing, pondering, trying to absorb the fact that such trees could really exist. Never before had I visited a national park where everyone was sitting silently in meditation: savoring, waking up to wonder, and offering homage to something truly magnificent that had lived so long.

As I walked reverently through a grove of sequoias, I wasn't surprised to read a plaque attached to one mammoth stump informing me that in the 1800s a Sunday school teacher had taught her entire class on the colossal base of that stump. Apparently worship among these trees has been going on for a long time. Strolling back toward the parking lot and toward the final grove of sequoias, I encountered an actual worship service in session, but it wasn't Sunday morning. Kneeling at the trunk of one giant tree, at noon on a Saturday, were ten Latino worshipers singing quietly in Spanish, hands folded in prayer. That must be the summons of the giant sequoia: to stop whatever you're doing and to pray, to kneel on the earth in reverence and wonder.

When you see a fawn or a cormorant or a blossoming pear tree, when you smell a fresh lemon or a ripe peach or a honeysuckle blossom, when you touch the fur of a puppy or the petal of a rose or the spiral of a seashell, when you hear the cry of a loon or the crash of a wave or the hush of a soft wind in the pines, wonder—all around—invites you in.

Treasure your friendships

For eleven years my friend Kathleen and I took a one-hour walk every two weeks, rarely missing that appointment. Activist Nelle Morton reminds us that "we hear each other into speech."[10] In 2008, to my great desolation, Kathleen moved halfway across the country, and we both found ourselves bereft at the loss of our routine. Those many years we thought we were meeting to walk, we actually met to listen. Each year we took more and more risks in our friendship until eventually we could talk about almost anything in the safe haven we had created for one another.

On the side of one of the great temples in Egypt are two large, carved ears. They're displayed on a section of the temple devoted to "the healing arts." And the ears are appropriate, because a significant part of the healing process is achieved when we are truly heard. In my spiritual direction room, I have a framed image on papyrus of those two large, carved ears. When I meet with the men and women coming to me for spiritual guidance, I'm reminded of the healing power of listening. As we remain silent, attentively listening to a friend, it helps to remember that *silent* and *listen* are made up of precisely the same letters, words that go hand in hand.

One important part of the savoring of friendship is listening; another part is letting others know they aren't taken for granted. I make frequent trips to Office Depot—my second home—purchasing folders, stocking up on paper, buying nametags, and making copies. The staff there has become almost a second family, sharing their latest news with me and proudly showing me pictures of children and grandchildren. My life is made infinitely richer by their assistance and their kindness. Pondering what I could do to let my helpers know I didn't take them for granted, I decided to bake the family favorite, Scotcheroos: peanut butter and chocolate Rice Krispies treats. When I made my delivery, I told them, "You all make my life so much easier. Thank you!" A little later, in the middle of my photocopying, one of the employees came up to me, a Scotcheroo dangling from his mouth. "Did you make these?" he asked.

"Yes, I did," I replied.

"Will you marry me?" he jokingly asked, letting me know we find friendship and deepen connection when we let others know how much we appreciate them.

If you treasure a friendship, say so. Be bold and tell someone you love them. You never know how much time either of you has left to say what's important. On September 24, 2007, my dear friend Brenda died of a brain tumor. She had been my closest friend in Milwaukee when she was a United Church of Christ pastor in nearby West Bend. At the time we met, we both were new to Wisconsin and to the churches we served. We shared many things in common—we even discovered that we had lived just a mile apart in Columbus, Ohio, when we were young. She was a compassionate and loving human being—a deep thinker, a constant seeker—and she stretched me. She also made me laugh—often. On countless occasions when I was her roommate at tedious denominational meetings, we would stay up talking late into the night. Brenda was the one who taught me to say "I love you" to my friends. Once, as we were finishing a phone conversation, she said, "I love you, Holly." That startled me into quiet, but she continued, "You know, we have to tell our friends that we love them. Life's too short to let things go and not tell our friends how precious they are to us."

Practices and Ponderings

A First Spiritual Practice of Finding: Savoring Beauty

"As I grow older, . . . my life is filled with more moments of joy," writes psychologist Mary Pipher. "Even when I am in deep pain, I can rescue myself by noticing a small beautiful thing. A golden leaf turning in a cobweb or the smell of a gardenia can stop me in my tracks. Heaven is all around me just waiting for me to notice."[11] The presence of beauty restores, heals, and leads us to wonder.

Choose a particular day on which you will make yourself aware of beauty three times: in the morning, in the afternoon, and in the evening. Notice the impact this has on your perspective. Do you feel more joyful? More grateful? If so, you might want to make this practice a daily one.

A Second Spiritual Practice of Finding: Savoring God

Sit somewhere comfortable and light a candle if you wish. Settle in and breathe in and out slowly. Savor God (or the Divine or the Holy One or your favorite name for God). Reflect on what that relationship has provided. Constancy? Comfort? Unconditional love? In the spirit of finding, see what arises.

Questions to Ponder

Slow down and pay attention

- At what pace do you live your life? How would you benefit from slowing down?
- What simple pleasures do you value? How do they bring you joy?
- What do you most recently remember savoring?

Dwell in the fullness of time

- Savoring the present: What, for you personally, are the advantages of living fully in the present?
- Savoring the past: What good memories do you savor over and over again?
- Savoring the future: What are you most looking forward to right now? How can you savor that anticipation and allow it to bring you delight?

Wake up to wonder

- How are you making space for wonder? What most recently took your breath away?

- For you, how is wonder connected to God?
- What moments of reverence or transcendence have you experienced in the last few months?
- When were you most recently nourished by nature or the presence of beauty?

Treasure your friendships

- Who has listened attentively to you? How is this part of your health or healing?
- How do you savor your friends?
- How do you nurture your friendships?

Chapter Two

Finding Vulnerability through Saying Yes

Whenever we're beset by conflict or adversity or change, our first reaction is likely to be "Oh, no!" That response closes us down and invites despair. It shuts off possibility and leads us into a mire of self-pity and dejection. Author and therapist Carolyn Hobbs writes, "Think of something in your life that you're not too happy about—perhaps an altercation, a health issue, something you wish hadn't appeared at all. Without any judgment, notice your first reaction. Then try saying 'Yes' to this situation. Notice what happens inside you as you do this."[1] "Oh, yes!" clears a path for vulnerability and uncertainty, and also for newness, gratitude, and hope.

In improvisational comedy, players are instructed to always say Yes, to play off the line the previous actor has thrown their way. Saying No instantly grinds interaction to a halt, and the stage becomes silent. That's why improv actors always say Yes, even though the scene can become dicey and they can become vulnerable. When they continue saying Yes, the comedy becomes larger and funnier, and the dialogue continues.

When we practice saying Yes, even when it's hard, it changes everything. Here are some powerful ways to say Yes.

Say Yes to being vulnerable to something larger than yourself

Every once in a while, each of us participates in something that makes us bigger, that broadens us, that helps us to realize that we're part of a larger whole. This expands our perspective and increases our sense of connection and purpose. Such experiences are valuable because they teach us to be less insular and less self-absorbed. When I've joined with others to sing with the dying in hospice care, to participate in hunger walks, and to feed the poor at an urban meal program, I've taken pleasure in being part of something larger than myself.

In January of 2012, I began volunteering at The Gathering, a soup kitchen in the inner city of Milwaukee, because I wanted to have more diversity in my life and to understand better the social issues of people in that part of my city. The soup kitchen is in a church where I circulate among the guests every other Wednesday night.

Why do I volunteer? Because I can nourish and be nourished. When I put on my apron, suddenly I'm at ease and relaxed, loved and cared for in the jostle of humanity. Serving here is one of my favorite activities. Yes, I have to be vulnerable over and over again, but this welcoming place with its abundant rewards encourages me to say Yes to something larger than myself.

A couple of months ago, another volunteer colleague told me, "I come here because it's a happy place, and I need happy." You might not guess that a dining room for the poor and homeless would necessarily be a happy place, but it's a place of respite and rest, of community and acceptance, of sanctuary. There's a lot of talking, a lot of laughing, a lot of kidding around. Recently, one homeless man, looking at me with a twinkle in his eye, offered a backhanded compliment: "You must have been cute when you were young." The Gathering is a happy place because people receive food for their bodies and kindness for their souls. When people enter, they look for their friends and save seats for one another—even as newcomers are welcomed in.

Another bounty I receive when I volunteer there is that I can be myself. In my professional life, especially at public events, there is a need to be constantly "on":

credible, smooth, self-asserting—and that gets to be wearying. At this meal site, I simply show up, put on my apron, and start moving among the guests.

The Gathering has also taught me a new benediction, a new farewell. Usually when I part from a person, I say "Take care." The farewell greeting at The Gathering is not "Take care" but "Stay safe." The streets of the near south side can be tough, and "Stay safe" is a compassionate blessing to offer.

The community that gathers in that room to eat represents the great melting pot of humanity. We meet folks who must choose between buying groceries or purchasing medicine or paying rent. Some people are homeless; some are employed full-time. Some folks are coping with alcoholism, drug dependence, or mental illness. Some are ex-convicts or pedophiles or have warrants out for their arrest. Most of the guests are men, but there are a considerable number of women and children. We who are volunteers are varied too: men, women, children, Christians, Hindus, Muslims. Our common denominator at this wild and wonderful soup kitchen is that we are all needy and we are all nourished.

Another rich blessing I receive is that my *imago dei*, or image of God, is always changing. I'm learning to see the face of Christ in more and more places. Jesus pops up when I least expect him.

When volunteers first come to help at this meal program, they're given a little preparatory talk by Jim, a retired homicide cop and the program coordinator. Jim is a gentle but firm man, street smart and expansively kind. Jim explains to new volunteers the sacred work of feeding people in a dining room that is a "no judgment zone." Each guest is to be treated with respect and dignity. Each guest is to be treated like Christ himself.

The face of Christ is always changing. From time to time one of the more flamboyant prostitutes comes in. When I saw a particular prostitute a couple of months ago, she was strung out and very combative. Some of us are a bit wary of her because she can become quarrelsome quickly. But we all have empathy because her life is impossible in every conceivable way. Not long ago I recognized her immediately in the food line. She was hard to miss: synthetic fur coat, false eyelashes, and big wig. Even harder to miss were her black stockings and five-inch bright-gold stiletto heels. I brought her a beverage and was relieved that she wasn't argumentative and difficult. After she put down her tray, I watched as she got settled. She slung her big coat over the chair, sat down, and folded her hands as she bowed her head. She prayed—for a long time—before she ate. I stared at her, stunned. And then, against my will, I started to cry. Sometimes God reveals the holy to us when we least expect it. Sometimes our stereotypes are blown away. Often the face of Jesus will appear in a guise we don't want to embrace. This may happen when we're willing to say Yes to being vulnerable to something larger than ourselves.

Say Yes to being vulnerable as God is vulnerable

The incarnation, part of the Christian story, astonishes me. The first chapter of the Gospel of John says, "The Word became flesh and lived among us." What does this mean? God human, God assailable, God laid bare. As I'm growing older and becoming more vulnerable, my strength and stamina are waning a bit. I'm pretty useless after seven at night. I don't have the fortitude and confidence I possessed when I was younger. Now more than ever, I appreciate the vulnerability of God. Writer Melissa Tidwell elaborates on the Word becoming flesh when she says, "It is staggering to consider God's willingness to accept—or even God's desire to experience—a human form, living in a body like ours. It opens us up to marvel at the idea of a perfect, eternal God becoming perishable, harmable, capable of grief and pain, and, finally, death."[2] The word "incarnation" comes from the Latin verb *incarnare*, which means "to make into flesh."

How do we wrap our minds around incarnation and a vulnerable God? Author and food pantry director Sara Miles writes, "This was where I found my faith: a faith expressed in the wild conceit that a helpless, low-caste baby could be God. That ugly, contaminated people and unimportant people embodied holiness. That my own neediness and misfitting, not my goodness or piety, were what God intended to use."[3] As I read those words, I find myself comforted by this affirmation of faith, and I unconsciously exhale. These words serve as an antidote to my striving and remind me that I don't have to be perfect—that I am allowed to be vulnerable.

Most of us struggle with vulnerability. In our work or our personal lives we may be seduced by images of our virtue and personal power, thinking these will win us accolades or personal agency. But of course we all know on a deep level that it is in fact not our perfection but our humanness and our vulnerability that are the bridges to other people. Everybody finds us more approachable when we are flawed and human. God became human in the incarnation, and we become human when we are open and vulnerable and less than perfect. As Anne Lamott writes:

God sent Jesus to join the human experience, which means to make a lot of mistakes. Jesus didn't arrive here knowing how to walk. He had fingers and toes, confusion, sexual feelings, crazy human internal processes. He had the same prejudices as the rest of his tribe: he had to learn that the Canaanite woman was a person. He had to suffer the hardships and tedium and setbacks of being a regular person. If he hadn't the Incarnation would mean nothing.[4]

The incarnation is about God understanding our vulnerability and our humanness because Jesus is God with skin on, God entering the struggle, God vulnerable, God succeeding, God failing, God human. God came to earth to meet us where we are: through our best selves, through our worst selves, and in all our human yearnings.

Say Yes to your humanness

Teacher and writer Philip Simmons (1957–2002) taught literature and creative writing at Lake Forest College in Illinois. At age thirty-five, he was diagnosed with Lou Gehrig's disease, or ALS (amyotrophic lateral sclerosis). In his astute and tender volume of reflections, *Learning to Fall: The Blessings of an Imperfect Life*, he writes:

Our . . . challenge is to see God not only in the eyes of the suffering child but in the suffering itself. . . . To thank God for broken bones and broken hearts, for everything that opens us to the mystery of our humanness. The challenge is to stand at the sink with your hands in the dishwater, fuming over a quarrel with your spouse, children at your back clamoring for attention, the radio blatting . . . , and to say, "God is here, now, in this room, here in this dishwater, in this dirty spoon."[5]

When we begin to say Yes to both the exhilaration and the misery that make us human, we become more complicated and credible human beings. We start to understand that some of life's richest lessons come not from success and confidence but from the vulnerability of defeat and brokenness, conflict and disappointment. When I was a pastor in my twenties and early thirties, I thought I had to be perfect and invulnerable. It was challenging to be a female solo pastor in the 1970s and 1980s. I felt I had to responsibly inhabit the role of pastor every hour of every day. Few people had met a woman who was also a pastor, and I constantly experienced the burden of setting a good example in church, in the grocery store, in the lingerie department, at the dentist's office. In those times, I didn't have close friends. They were too intrusive, too risky, too dangerous. Those early years of ministry taught me well to keep my guard up. No one was going to see a chink in my armor and find me vulnerable. I hadn't yet learned to trust friends or develop confidantes, and the result was that I was frequently anxious, isolated, and depressed.

One of the great joys of growing older has been learning to be vulnerable. Looking at my earlier life from my vantage point now, I think, "What foolishness it was to have been so trapped and so lonely." I am so very grateful for my friends now, my tolerant friends who know and love me. I've developed close friendships and now live with much less seriousness and much more laughter. This has freed me enormously and also made me more approachable and more human.

In the summer of 1976, at age twenty-two, I had completed one year of seminary, and I was doing my first unit of CPE, or clinical pastoral education, at Yale New Haven Hospital. This educational requirement for seminarians is nothing less than spiritual boot camp. My first summer being a chaplain was a mind-boggling experience with a discerning and very tough supervisor. During that summer, it eventually came to be my turn to be the chaplain on call for all of Yale New Haven Hospital, in all of its immense fearsomeness. Petrified, I felt as if I would jump out of my skin if the on-call beeper went off. Sensing my panic, my supervisor told me bluntly to stop regarding the beeper as if it were the Ark of the Covenant and to get a grip on myself. Though young, inexperienced, and afraid, I survived my first trial by fire that on-call night and became a little more confident.

Then one afternoon revered theologian Henri Nouwen came over from the seminary to teach our CPE group as a guest lecturer. I had seen Nouwen on campus at Yale Divinity School but had not yet taken classes with him. The well-known author of *The Wounded Healer*, he told our class that day that we didn't have to be anxious. This was a huge balm to my quaking soul. "You have everything you need," he said. "You are enough. You simply walk into each hospital room with a spirit of compassion, receptivity, and your open hands." All you need is your humanness, Nouwen told us that day. Trust that and see what happens. This is the surprising good news: we are human, vulnerable, imperfect, and that is enough.

Practices and Ponderings

A First Spiritual Practice of Finding:
Say Yes to Taking Risks and Learning to Change

When we take risks and are willing to change, we become vulnerable. It's hard, but the rewards are enormous. Try this exercise from Philippa Perry:

> Get a large piece of plain paper and draw a circle in the middle. Inside the circle write examples of activities that you feel completely comfortable doing. Around the edge of the circle, write down examples of activities that you can do but that you have to push yourself a little bit to do—those activities that may make you nervous in some way, but not so much as to stop you doing them. Draw a larger circle around this circle of activities. In the next band write down activities that you would like to do but find it difficult to get up the courage *to* do. Draw another circle around this ring of activities. After that write down those things you are far too scared to try but would like to do. You can create as many circles as you like.[6]

The challenge—trying some of the "outer circle" activities—is scary but rewarding. Vulnerability results in growth, maturity, and change. And growing is contagious; the more we risk, the more confidence we bring to risking more. Developing our ability to change matures us and offers us resilience and wisdom. How are you saying Yes to change? What risks have stretched you? What new skill are you proud to have recently learned?

A Second Spiritual Practice of Finding:
Breathe in Yes, Breathe out Thanks

The practice of finding reminds us to say Yes to our lives—and to say thanks. Dag Hammarskjöld, United Nations Secretary-General and Nobel Peace Prize winner, wrote: "For all that has been, thanks. To all that will be, yes."[7] Thich Nhat Hanh writes in the same vein: "At Plum Village, I teach the young people a simple verse to practice while walking. '*Oui, oui, oui*,' as they breathe in, and '*Merci, merci, merci*,' as they breathe out. 'Yes, yes, yes. Thanks, thanks, thanks.' I want them to respond to life, to society, and to the Earth in a positive way."[8]

Try this spiritual breath exercise as a kind of prayer that you say several times a day.

Breathe in: Yes, yes, yes.
Breathe out: Thanks, thanks, thanks.

Try this for one week. Can you feel a difference?

Questions to Ponder

Say Yes to being vulnerable to something larger than yourself

- What experiences have you said Yes to that have stretched you?
- How have you let yourself be vulnerable through these experiences?
- How have you become bolder through having said Yes?

Say Yes to being vulnerable as God is vulnerable

- How do you see the incarnate God, Jesus, as being vulnerable?
- How has Jesus taught you by his vulnerability?
- How did Jesus find vulnerability through saying Yes?
- How are you finding vulnerability through saying Yes?

Say Yes to your humanness

- ❧ How are you saying Yes to your humanness and your frailties?
- ❧ How are you being tender and forgiving to yourself?
- ❧ How are you saying "I am enough"?
- ❧ Where is God's invitation here?

Chapter Three

Reaching beyond Suffering and Finding Resilience

"Don't waste your suffering!" someone once told me. This admonition propelled me to accept suffering and learn from it. Suffering bestows an abundance of hard-won insights and a strange new confidence in our toughness, creating a rich reservoir of maturity. We don't become wise and multifaceted human beings until we suffer. Rob Bell cautions: "Don't rush through the experiences and circumstances that have the most capacity to transform you."[1] It seems strange to think of sorrow as a catalyst for the practice of finding, but that's what it is. Some lessons are learned no other way.

There is not one of us who has lived past middle age who has not resonated with the words of the Psalms, particularly the sorrowful words of Psalm 6: "Be gracious to me, O Lord, for I am languishing: / O Lord, heal me, for my bones are shaking with terror. / My soul also is struck with terror, / while you, O Lord—how long? . . . I am weary with my moaning; / every night I flood my bed with tears; / I drench my couch with my weeping." Suffering is universal and inescapable. None of us will be spared. There is a saying, often attributed to Chinua Achebe, that goes: "When suffering knocks at your door and you say there is no seat for him, he tells you not to worry because he has brought his own stool." Suffering walks in, takes a seat, and makes itself at home in all of our lives. Buddhists remind us that there are ten thousand joys and ten thousand sorrows. Each of us suffers differently, yet we share a common experience of grief and loss. We also share a desire to grow from our suffering and to redeem it if we can.

This is not to suggest that we endure hardship in order to immediately give thanks for the deepening of our character. Sometimes a full understanding of the lessons of sorrow takes thirty or forty years. Over time, and sometimes lots of time, we eventually become richer, more compassionate through our suffering. Richard Rohr says, "Losing, failing, falling, sin, and the suffering that comes from those experiences— all of this is a necessary and even good part of the human journey."[2] And from author and psychologist Mary Pipher we hear these words:

> We all have within us the capacity not only to heal from crises but also to turn our sorrow into some-

thing new and strong. In fact, true growth requires spending time outside one's comfort zone. Happiness need not be analyzed. Comfortable people tend to cling to their old patterns. Indeed, adults who have never suffered are shallow and, well, insufferable. Because they haven't experienced much pain, they haven't felt motivated to try to explore themselves and their relationships to the world.[3]

How do we begin? Sometimes it's as basic as asking ourselves if we're willing to give this a try, willing to reach beyond our suffering to find resilience.

Don't waste your suffering

Because it expresses human incredulity so very well, one of my favorite Bible stories is of the Annunciation, recorded in the Gospel of Luke (1:26–34):

In the sixth month the angel Gabriel was sent by God to a town in Galilee called Nazareth, to a virgin engaged to a man whose name was Joseph, of the house of David. The virgin's name was Mary. And he came to her and said, "Greetings, favored one! The Lord is with you." But she was much perplexed by his words and pondered what sort of greeting this might be. The angel said to her, "Do not be afraid, Mary, for you have found favor with God. And now, you will conceive in your womb and bear a son, and you will name him Jesus. He will be great, and will be called the Son of the Most High, and the Lord God will give to him the throne of his ancestor David. He will reign over the house of Jacob forever, and of his kingdom there will be no end." Mary said to the angel, "How can this be, since I am a virgin?"

In this scripture, the young girl Mary experiences what writer Mark Nepo calls an "unplanned unfolding."[4] Some unplanned unfoldings are wondrous and good, like having your best friend move back to town. Others are minor curveballs, like having a bad blind date. And then there are some that change our lives forever—and that's precisely what's going on here with Mary.

The Gospel of Luke illustrates a major disorienting event for this teenager. And her challenging unplanned unfolding, like all of ours, is disturbing, messy, perplexing—and unbelievable. In her particular circumstance, Mary says to the angel Gabriel, "I can't believe I'll have a baby when I'm still a virgin!" Like Mary, we are confronted with our own scenarios that seem to us unbelievable, unplanned unfoldings that are your stories or my stories or the stories of our friends.

I can't believe my child got cancer. We live in a green, non-toxic house, and we eat only organic food and drink organic milk.

I can't believe my husband left me for someone else. I was always faithful to him, and I tried hard to tend to his needs.

I can't believe I was fired after thirty-eight years. I was vigilantly pro-active; I kept up with all the company's developments, performing consistently and well. I learned all the technological updates the company required. I can't believe they let me go.

I can't believe my mom was assaulted when she was coming out of work. She's a nurse on second shift, and she was opening her car door in the parking garage when they grabbed her.

I can't believe my daughter has dementia. She's only forty-nine. She doesn't have metabolic syndrome, and dementia doesn't run in our family.

Our unplanned unfoldings are much like Mary's. We don't see them coming. They contradict our understanding of what was believable and what we had come to count on. For months or years, we ask, "How can I accept what has happened to me as being true?" For a long time we remain incredulous and stunned. Usually this experience stretches us in every way. Maybe we've come out of several unplanned unfoldings and are now experiencing the fruits of survival and maturity on the other side. Friedrich Nietzsche said, "What doesn't kill you makes you stronger."[5] Comedian Conan O'Brien offers a little midrash on Nietzsche when he says, "What doesn't kill you almost kills you."[6] That's the way unplanned unfoldings are. They just about kill us, but then we survive. We learn new things that we didn't even want to learn. We become stronger in spite of ourselves. We find ourselves disoriented, but anchored in place.

Perhaps Barbara Brown Taylor describes unplanned unfoldings best:

> In my life, I have lost my way more times than I can count. I have set out to be married and ended up divorced. I have set out to be healthy and ended up sick. I have set out to live in New England, and ended up in Georgia. When I was thirty, I set out to be a parish priest, planning to spend the rest of my life caring for souls in any congregation that would have me. Almost thirty years later, I teach school.
>
> While none of these displacements was pleasant at first, I would not give a single one of them back. I

have found things while I was lost that I might never have discovered if I had stayed on the path.[7]

If we embrace our unplanned unfoldings, as hard as it is, we won't waste our suffering. We can value our survival tactics as the currency of maturity and can affirm that what we've gleaned through pain is gold. As I have struggled through my own such unfoldings, I've learned some invaluable lessons, which I now pass on to you.

1. Accept that you can't figure certain things out and that there are some things you'll never know. This is one of the hardest parts of unplanned unfoldings, the not-knowing. When we get stuck in unpredictable circumstances, we want to know why: Why did my child get sick? Why did my husband leave? Why did I lose my job? Sometimes we do know the answers to questions like these, but often we never will. There are huge pieces of our lives that we will have to let go of ever understanding. This is very difficult, especially at first. Often we want to keep picking at these wounds, thinking that if we keep at it, then we will find answers, then something will come clear. But often it doesn't. Our picking at our wounds only increases the cyclical thinking, the obsessing, the perseverating. We may never know why our crisis has happened, and for our own sanity, we need to learn to live in the

not-knowing. The eventual acceptance of not knowing is an enormous spiritual leap, and it is here that
we depend on God. When our not knowing drives us
crazy, we offer it up and ask God for comfort. In the
process of letting go, the Serenity Prayer often helps.
I pray it all the time.

> God, grant me the serenity to accept the things I
>   cannot change,
> Courage to change the things I can,
> And wisdom to know the difference.[8]

2. Find friends and accept their help. When unplanned unfoldings undo us, we can't navigate them
alone. We need to be held up or carried for a while. Several unplanned unfoldings in my life taught me repeat-
edly that I must learn to receive. Too often I've been a
proud, lonely, caregiving person, and it has been my unplanned unfoldings that have brought me to my knees
and have also taught me to receive and deepen friendship. Over time I have learned to make space for friends
and to meet them for weekends or walks or lunch or
coffee. With these grace-filled, forgiving, truth-telling
friends, I tell my story and listen to their stories. We
laugh, we cry, and they give it to me straight.

3. Know that reorientation will take time. When
unplanned unfoldings come our way, we need time—

lots and lots of time. We mustn't allow ourselves to be rushed or to be victims of others' expectations, or to be labeled inadequate or malingering if we don't heal on a prescribed schedule. Whether we've experienced loss or displacement or trauma, we don't adjust to changed circumstances quickly. That reorientation may take six months or two years or a decade. And in the case of trauma, healing is not predictably linear. Healing after trauma may be a few steps forward and a few steps back. Poet Antonio Machado writes: "Anyone who moves forward, even a little, is like Jesus walking on the water."[9] Sadly, our culture is not particularly supportive of persons in shock or grief. So we need to realistically claim adequate time for our healing and reorientation.

4. Trust that you are actually tougher than you give yourself credit for. Sometimes we think we can get through only a few months of depression or anxiety or loss, only to discover that we can make it through much longer periods. And there is a certain credibility and confidence that come from being tested and becoming stronger. Remember during the anguish of unplanned unfoldings that you will see life and light again. Your misery won't last for eternity. Things won't always be this hard.

5. Let yourself be distracted. I have found this to be very helpful. If one area of your life is tough

and unpredictable and sad, try looking at the other parts. If you discover activities that bring you joy for a while, let yourself participate in those. They'll give you much-needed rest from your anxiety or pain. Perhaps you'd enjoy reading a compelling novel, or eating lunch with a friend, or going to the movies. Embracing these distractions can give your life better balance and help you handle the hard part.

6. Embrace gratitude and give thanks. Even in the midst of unplanned unfoldings, it helps to stop and be grateful for something, however small, that is peaceful or lovely or running smoothly. When we are shocked and made vulnerable by an unplanned unfolding, our broken-open hearts teach us to consider the blessing of small things we wouldn't have noticed before. In our fragility, little things become a lifeline: the affectionate greeting of a dog or cat at the front door, the food a neighbor has left on the porch, a peaceful sit in a lilac-filled park, a gentle touch of understanding, a homemade card from a child. Even in the midst of tribulation and trouble, the practice of finding allows us to lift our heads.

7. Consider the notion that "despair is presumptuous."[10] I first came across this idea a few years ago from Episcopal priest John Claypool. In the midst of my unplanned unfoldings, I remained unconvinced of this notion because it seemed arrogant and false.

And yet, the longer I've lived and the more I've survived, the more I comprehend the truth of this statement. There have been a number of times in my life when I've thought that light and healing were impossible, and yet, over months and sometimes years, those things came to me. When I thought that I would drown in my despair, light and healing dawned in the form of a trusted friend, a skilled therapist, or an unexpected affirmation. Perhaps despair is presumptuous after all.

Unplanned unfoldings will continue to disrupt our lives because we're vulnerable human beings. Just as they happened to Mary, they will happen to all of us. What we need to remember is that our deepest pain may also lead to our deepest transformation.

Take pride in your strength

Suffering stretches us and makes demands on us. Suffering requires us to dig deeply and to pull forth more from ourselves than we thought possible.

Elizabeth Lesser, in her magnificent book *Broken Open*, describes a scene from one of her workshops. It is the end of a long day of inner work. One of the participants, a woman overcome by anger and regret, begins to cry. Lesser writes:

When I turned the lights back on, an elderly woman who had said little during the workshop's first two days rose and raised her hand, as if she were in grade school. She had a refined and almost translucent face and was dressed in a tailored blue wool suit, in contrast to the sweatpants and T-shirts most people were wearing. . . . I sensed that the workshop angel had arrived.

"May I say something, dear?" she asked me.

"Of course," I said.

"I am ninety-two years old." She chuckled. Everyone gasped. She was such an elegant and energetic woman—that no one would have correctly guessed her age.

"I am speaking to all of you, but especially to you," she said with great warmth, acknowledging the angry woman, who was seated across the circle. "I've had a life of adventures and a life of losses. I've lost two husbands and a son. But at ninety-two, as hard as I try, I can't find anything to be unhappy about! I know now that all of my difficulties made me who I am supposed to be."

Now she leaned forward and looked straight at the angry woman. "Do you know the poet Rainer Maria Rilke, dear? He wrote a poem that ends like this: 'In the difficult are the friendly forces, the hands that work on us.' Isn't that wonderful? Our problems are friendly! They are like hands that want to work on us. They want to make us strong. They certainly worked on me! Now, even though I am an old woman, I am stronger than ever."[11]

As we ponder our friendly forces and offer thanks for the times we've found our strength, we learn to value every morsel of healing that comes our way. After emotional trauma or physical injury, healing is measured in halting steps. The whole process of recovery is arduous and requires a great deal of patience, but we help ourselves when we notice the healing that takes place every day, every week, every month, or maybe even in this very moment. Anne Lamott writes, "[I]f you've been around for a while, you know that much of the time, if you are patient and are paying attention, you will see that God will restore what the locusts have taken away."[12]

Claim your resilience

Resilience is our ability to eventually bounce back after loss or terror or attack or betrayal. For decades, psychologist Dr. Julius Segal has studied particular groups of traumatized persons: refugees, prisoners of war, hostages, and concentration camp survivors. He has also studied ordinary people who have been assaulted, who have been in debilitating accidents, or whose children are struggling with cancer. He has discovered that most of us are much more resilient than we think. After examining my own suffering, I realized that for years I had subconsciously been digging myself out of distress by practicing resilience—although I didn't know to call it that. Most of us who achieve resilience have practiced being resilient, knowingly or unknowingly, in the following ways:[13]

- We confide and communicate. When traumatized and desperate, we cultivate resilience by reaching out and telling our story. Telling our story affirms our worthiness and our truth. The process of sharing and being taken seriously builds resilience.
- We take charge rather than remaining hopeless or passive. We practice resilience by taking control of our circumstances instead of submitting to a learned helplessness. One Iranian hostage shared with Dr. Segal that the simple discipline of shaving each day during his fourteen months of captivity helped him to preserve his sense of autonomy and control.
- We give purpose to our pain. Dr. Segal tells the story of Eileen Stevens, whose twenty-year-old son, Chuck, died after a fraternity hazing during

which he was locked in the trunk of a car and forced to drink large amounts of alcohol. In order to find meaning after her child's unnecessary death, Stevens founded C.H.U.C.K.: Committee to Halt Useless College Killings. She has made it her mission to speak to fraternities all around the country and to help pass state laws prohibiting the kind of hazing that took her son's life. This bereft mother channeled her grief and rage into positive purpose.

· We lessen the burden of self-blame. In the midst of crisis and trauma, we often blame ourselves for not being perfect or all-knowing. "If only I hadn't driven through that yellow light." "If only I hadn't let her go to that sleepover." "If only I had insisted that the doctor take me seriously." "If only I hadn't been an innocent child when it happened." Sooner or later we grasp that blaming ourselves is an obstacle to our resilience because it isolates us from other people and results in our relentless rumination.

· We heal ourselves through helping and inspiring others. We practice resilience by eventually becoming less self-absorbed and by reaching out to others in pain, by overcoming our devastation and demonstrating courage to our children or to other survivors. Reaching beyond our own wounded selves energizes others and increases our own confidence. Alcoholics Anonymous is so successful not just because of the psychological good sense of the Twelve Steps, but because folks listen, support, and guide one another in AA meetings and other contexts.

Part of claiming resilience is learning to redeem what has happened. Words associated with the verb "redeem" are "recover," "release," "restore." In my own life, when I have been able to redeem my pain, when I have been able to receive a gift of insight from it, my healing has gone much better. When we redeem something in a spiritual sense, we buy it back in our own unique way. We make some kind of sense of it. We generate learning from it.

Wendell Berry, a Kentucky farmer, is one of our greatest living American poets. Like Jesus, he often relies on agricultural images as metaphors in his teaching. Here he writes eloquently of the resilience of an old, scarred sycamore tree, which can serve as a metaphor for our own scarred selves.

The Sycamore

In the place that is my own place, whose earth
I am shaped in and must bear, there is an old tree
    growing,
a great sycamore that is a wondrous healer of itself.
Fences have been tied to it, nails driven into it,
hacks and whittles cut in it, the lightning has
    burned it.
There is no year it has flourished in
that has not harmed it. There is a hollow in it
that is its death, though its living brims whitely
at the lip of the darkness and flows outward.
Over all its scars has come the seamless white
of the bark. It bears the gnarls of its history
healed over. It has risen to a strange perfection
in the warp and bending of its long growth.
It has gathered all accidents into its purpose.
It has become the intention and radiance of its dark
    fate.
It is a fact, sublime, mystical and unassailable.
In all the country, there is no other like it.
I recognize in it a principle, an indwelling
the same as itself, and greater, that I would be ruled
    by.
I see that it stands in its place, and feeds upon it,
and is fed upon, and is native, and maker.[14]

Engage your broken heart

There are precious lessons that only a broken heart can learn. Brokenheartedness is a wide window to empathy and clear-sightedness. The willingness to attend to the curriculum of a broken heart can propel us down a path that redeems our suffering. Ben Zander, conductor of the Boston Philharmonic Orchestra, offers these insights into a broken heart:

> [I] once had a distraught young tenor ask to speak to me after class. He told me he'd lost his girlfriend and was in such despair that he was almost unable to function. I consoled him, but the teacher in me was secretly delighted. Now he would be able to fully express the heartrending passion of the song in Schubert's *Die Winterreise* about the loss of the beloved. That song had completely eluded him the previous week because up to then, the only object of affection he had ever lost was a pet goldfish.
>
> My teacher, the great cellist Gaspar Cassadó, used to say to us as students, "I'm so sorry for you; your lives have been so easy. You can't play great music unless your heart's been broken."[15]

A broken heart is actually a full heart. When we're separated from someone we love, we yearn to be back in their presence. When we lose someone we love through death, our hearts break because we miss them so. Sadness and thanksgiving, grief and praise go hand in hand when we lose a loved one. There is a terror about this kind of deep loss, but we also have a sense of preciousness and gratitude that we were granted this depth of loving in the first place.

Etty Hillesum, a young Dutchwoman who was one of the most heroic diarists of the Holocaust, died in Auschwitz in 1943 at the age of twenty-nine. "Most people here," she writes, "are much worse off than they need be because they write off their longing for friends and family as so many losses in their lives, when they should count the fact that their heart is able to long so hard and to love so much among their greatest blessings."[16] A heart cannot be broken unless it is a heart full of love. When we learn to count our longings as a blessing, we have learned a profound lesson of love.

On March 12, 2004, my church, Redeemer United Church of Christ in Sussex, Wisconsin, burned to the ground. It was a grim and terrible night as members of the congregation watched helplessly while eighty-one firefighters from thirteen departments used 375,000 gallons of water in their efforts to extinguish the blaze. By morning, the persevering firefighters were overwhelmed by fatigue and emotionally defeated.

The charred remains looked like the city of London during the Blitz, a dreadful, ghostly, burned-out shell. We were all in shock that a random electrical fire had destroyed the building and all of its contents. We had lost the church we loved.

Or so we thought. But we didn't lose the church. We lost only the building. Our brokenheartedness had led to our clear-sightedness. We still had one another, and that was a powerful lesson. For quite a while after the fire, we lost interest in small or trivial concerns and didn't quibble about inconsequential material possessions. This offered us new perspective and held us—*the church*—steady for a long time.

Practices and Ponderings

A First Spiritual Practice of Finding:
What Suffering Has Taught Me

Create a stream-of-consciousness list called "What Suffering Has Taught Me." Take time to recall the losses and disappointments you've known. Does anything on this list surprise you? How does this list help you to reach beyond your suffering to find resilience? Are you in any small way ready to approach this list with gratitude?

A Second Spiritual Practice of Finding: Bitter or Better?

Retired Presbyterian pastor Bob Yoder poignantly recalls, "Once a dear parishioner who was homebound and had lived a life with a demanding husband and cared for an equally demanding mother-in-law told me, 'Bob, there is one letter difference in the words *bitter* and *better*. The way you face troubles will make you one or the other.'"[17] Bitter or better? How have you faced your troubles? What wisdom lies here for you?

Questions to Ponder

Don't waste your suffering

- ✿ In what ways have you used your suffering? What have you learned?
- ✿ How have your unplanned unfoldings become your teachers?

Take pride in your strength

- ✿ How has your suffering made you strong? How did this come about?
- ✿ What particular morsels of healing do you remember?

Claim your resilience

- ୬ Consider your life and the obstacles you've faced. What were those obstacles, and what resources did you call upon to overcome them?
- ୬ How have you been able to give purpose to your pain?
- ୬ Return to Wendell Berry's poem "The Sycamore" and read it again. How are you like that old tree? What wounds have you received? What wounds have you redeemed?

Engage your broken heart

- ୬ How has your broken heart been your teacher?
- ୬ How has your broken heart helped you to value the love you have known?

CHAPTER FOUR

Welcoming the Spirit and Finding Relationship with God

Lately the idea of God as Friend is something I've pondered, as well as what friendship with God might be deepening in my own life. Twelfth-century monk Aelred of Rievaulx says, "God is friendship," and fifth-century bishop Theodoret of Cyrus reminds us that "friendship with God is the entire goal of the Christian life."[1] But what does it mean to be a friend of God? What give-and-take does that require? In my experience, it requires three things.

Let God in

Most of us know well how to nurture human friendships and the kind of commitment they demand. We're good at sending texts or e-mails to arrange a cup of coffee or a walk or a meal. We enthusiastically make time for these get-togethers and understand the mutuality that friendship requires, some talking and some listening. Do we make time for God as we would for one of our friends? Do we put "God as Friend" on our daily or weekly calendar? Cardinal Basil Hume says,

> Each of us needs an opportunity to be alone,
> and silent,
> to find space in the day or in the week,
> just to reflect
> and to listen to the voice of God
> that speaks deep within us.
> Our search for God is only our response
> to [God's] search for us.
> [God] knocks at our door,
> but for many people their lives are too
> preoccupied
> for them to be able to hear.[2]

We let God in by making room for God. Schedule some time with God as Friend on your iPhone or mark God down in your datebook. Or simply sit in a chair, invite God in, and start breathing slowly and mindfully. (You really do know how to do this.) Just begin.

We also let God in by welcoming the movement of the Spirit. A while ago, I came across an old story in several newspapers. It continues to inspire me.[3]

On Friday, February 20, 1987, the only passenger on a small private plane—Ralph Flanders, from Tomah, Wisconsin—was mid-flight when the pilot suddenly stopped talking. Shortly after the single-engine Cessna took off from the Tomah airport, the pilot had suffered a heart attack, slumped over in his seat, and died. Flanders, a fifty-year-old insurance executive, made his way into the cockpit, grabbed the controls, and said to himself, "You better learn how to fly this right now," then picked up the radio microphone and called for help: "Mayday! Mayday! Mayday! Help! Help! Help! The pilot's dead. . . . I don't know how to fly a plane!"

Mike Feltz, a flight instructor who happened to be in the air with a student about fifty miles away, heard Flanders's call for help and flew toward the stranded passenger. Feltz coached him over the radio continuously, telling him what to do and trying to keep him calm. Flanders was piloting the Cessna for about an hour and a half, but said later, "It seemed like 125 million years or more." Eventually he made it back near Volk Field in Tomah, where the plane had taken off. The Cessna circled the airfield five or six times before landing. The first time the plane landed, it bounced back up into the air. On the next try, Flanders cut the throttle and landed the plane on the edge of the runway. He emerged from the plane shaken but uninjured.

With the heroic help of the young flight instructor who talked him through, Flanders landed the plane by himself. The real pilot lay dead on the seat beside him, and his own life had been saved.

This story stays with me for two reasons. First, it probably represents one of the worst scenarios that any of us can imagine. Second, and more importantly, this story embodies a profound analogy for the work of the Holy Spirit. We let God in when we notice what God is doing.

In the newspaper story, we hear of a man, stranded and desperate in mid-air, a man who has never flown a plane before in his life. And yet, he is calmed, reassured, and guided by a voice over a microphone. He is saved by an invisible co-pilot whose directions he follows with confidence and skill. The invisible co-pilot helps him to perform courageous acts he could never do by himself.

In a similar way, the Holy Spirit may walk beside us or hover over us, often interceding for us with sighs too deep for words. The Holy Spirit operates at the mystical interface of the spiritual world and our physical world, *companioning* us along. When our weakness or fear or lack of confidence overcomes us, the Spirit may act as co-pilot, talking us through the danger at hand and offering us strength we never knew we had. We let in God as Friend when we pay attention to the movement of the Spirit.

Trust God more

By the time we reach our fifties or sixties and have inevitably been tossed around by life, we increasingly comprehend how little control we have over much of anything. When I was young, I was under the illusion that I could control a lot. As I age, I realize that there is so much I can't know and can't predict. More and more now, I am surrendering, releasing, letting go. At last, I am trusting God more. Barbara Brown Taylor helps me to understand more deeply what trust in God is all about:

> In the same way that I am willing to thank my husband for a gift even before I have opened it—because I know him, because I trust his love of me, because I have faith we will survive even if he has given me a pneumatic nail gun for my birthday—I am willing to thank God for my life even before I know how it turns out. This is brave talk, I know, while I can still pay the bills, walk without assistance, and talk someone into going to the movies with me. My hope is that if I can practice saying thank you now, when I still approve of most of what is happening to me, then perhaps that practice will have become habit by the time I do not like much of anything that is happening to me. The plan is to replace approval

with gratitude. The plan is to take what *is* as God's ongoing answer to me.[4]

For some of us this is easy, for others grievously hard. But all of us find that we trust God more by learning to love whatever brings us closer to God. Sometimes the puzzlement is how to begin, and sometimes the process begins itself, as Ram Dass discovered one evening in 1997. Dass, a well-known spiritual teacher and the author of *Be Here Now*, sat on his bed trying to figure out how to end *Still Here*, his tenth book. As an active, athletic sixty-five-year-old, crazy about golf and surfing and joyfully traveling the country to make speaking engagements, he couldn't figure out how to communicate being older and closer to physical diminishment. But then his body gave him an answer: that night he suffered a terrible, debilitating stroke. "Three hospitals and hundreds of hours of rehabilitation later," he wrote, "I gradually eased into my new post-stroke life as someone in a wheelchair, partially paralyzed, requiring round-the-clock care and a degree of personal attention that made me uncomfortable." Later he added, "From the Ego's perspective the stroke is not much fun, from the Soul's perspective it's been a great learning opportunity."[5]

For years I have been challenged by what Ram Dass calls "fierce grace," the kind of grace to which we are led kicking and screaming, the kind of grace arising from circumstances we did not choose. Fierce grace comes only through adversity. "'Fierce grace' means I've been given a fully rounded understanding of grace," Dass says. "Now I have a full view of what grace is all about. . . . It's learning to love *whatever* it is that brings me closer to God."[6] One of our great spiritual masters, St. Francis, shares this lesson in a short poem:

In All Things

It was easy to love God in all that
was beautiful.
The lessons of deeper knowledge, though, instructed me
to embrace God in all
things.[7]

When we're in doubt and misery and slogging through a particularly dreadful chapter of our lives, it's hard to imagine that things will ever get better or that we'll gain perspective and knowledge from our trials. All we can see is our desperation and hopelessness. In these moments, we're just putting one foot in front of the other and simply surviving.

In such hard times, it can help us to remember that each of us possesses an "experiencing self" and a "remembering self."[8] If we find ourselves in a difficult stretch of life, our experiencing self is anxious, stressed, and traumatized. If we're eventually able to heal and to obtain some distance from our pain, our remembering self is less despairing and more hopeful. In other words, our experiencing self is smack dab in the middle of pain, feeling every agonizing pang. Our remembering self is less immediately involved and more forgiving because it's had a chance to heal and gain perspective. God is in the midst of all of this, helping us to move forward. The apostle Paul, in his first letter to the Corinthians, reminds us that we see "through a glass, darkly." And the refrain of the old gospel hymn "Farther Along" assures us that "we'll understand it all by and by," offering the long view, trusting that the end of the story may be better.

Even as we trust that the end may be better, we're also reminded that the events of life aren't always what they seem, as Anthony De Mello illustrates in this tale:

There is a Chinese story of an old farmer who had an old horse for tilling his fields. One day the horse escaped into the hills and when all the farmer's neighbors sympathized with the old man over his bad luck, the farmer replied, "Bad luck? Good luck? Who knows?" A week later the horse returned with a herd of wild horses from the hills and this time the neighbors congratulated the farmer on his good luck. His reply was, "Good luck? Bad luck? Who knows?" Then, when the farmer's son was attempting to tame one of the wild horses, he fell off its back and broke his leg. Everyone thought this very bad luck. Not the farmer, whose only reaction was, "Bad luck? Good luck? Who knows?" Some weeks later the army marched into the village and conscripted every able-bodied youth they found there. When they saw the farmer's son with his broken leg they let him off. Now was that good luck? Bad luck? Who knows?[9]

This parable reminds us of the fickleness of our premature judgments of all kinds. We never know the whole story. Orson Welles wrote: "If you want a happy ending, that depends, of course, on where you stop your story."[10] Frequently what we believe to be the end is only the middle. In our efforts to trust God more, it may serve us well to be aware of making judgments too quickly. This is far from easy and requires sustained determination. And can we, in the process, learn to trust the *end* of the story? If we can, we will grow to trust God more.

Embrace God's mercies

We grow in our friendship with God by consciously absorbing God's mercies. We live life more lightly and become more optimistic in the bargain. The practice of friendship and the practice of finding invite us to clothe ourselves with God's mercies each day, something Maya Angelou reflects on in a story about her grandmother "stepping out on the word of God":

> One of my earliest memories of Mamma, of my grandmother, is a glimpse of a tall cinnamon-colored woman with a deep, soft voice, standing thousands of feet up in the air on nothing visible. That incredible vision was a result of what my imagination would do each time Mamma drew herself up to her full six feet, clasped her hands behind her back, looked up into a distant sky, and said, "I will step out on the word of God."
>
> The depression, which was difficult for everyone, especially so for a single black woman in the South tending her crippled son and two grandchildren, caused her to make the statement of faith often.[11]

One way we practice an embrace of God's mercies is by remembering answered prayers, which transform and bless us. We mistakenly cling to and become obsessed with our unanswered prayers, missing a treasure trove of answered prayers to be lived into and cherished. Brother David Steindl-Rast, author of the gratitude classic *Gratefulness: The Heart of Prayer*, calls that kind of cherishing a "great fullness."[12] When we pause and remember our answered prayers, we experience that great fullness as well as an indescribable feeling that we have been loved and listened to. It's a touching exercise to recall our answered prayers and see what we discover. Look back to a year ago today. What were you praying about? Then review the past twelve months, remembering that answered prayer manifests itself in dozens of different ways. Has there been healing or assistance or resolution or clarity or reconciliation? When we take some time to stop and review, we open our hearts to what we uncover.

And how do we pray? An old adage reminds us that "the one who sings prays twice." When we sing, we may find ourselves praying with our bodies and spirits as well as our voices. My practice of finding God's mercies often takes the form of singing aloud this powerful, salvific verse from the hymn "Amazing Grace":

> Through many dangers, toils, and snares,
> I have already come;
> 'Tis grace has brought me safe thus far,
> and grace will lead me home.

These words help me remember answered prayers and deepen my trust in God. When I sing them, I recall once again all that God and I have survived together (*all* the dangers and toils and snares) and that God's grace will guide me home—whether that means home to myself or home back to God in death. This verse has comforted me and inspired me time and time again.

In the Outer Hebrides of Scotland, there is an ancient oral tradition of morning prayer. The morning prayer below encourages us to think of God as Friend and Lover and Source, and invites us to attentively remember the comprehensiveness of God's mercies:

> Each day may I remember the source of the
>   mercies
> Thou hast bestowed on me gently and generously;
> Each day may I be fuller in love to Thyself.
> *   *   *   *   *   *
> Each thing I have received, from Thee it came,
> Each thing for which I hope, from Thy love it will
>   come,
> Each thing I enjoy, it is of Thy bounty,
> Each thing I ask, comes of Thy disposing.[13]

Practices and Ponderings

A First Spiritual Practice of Finding: Try a Body Prayer

Try offering an out-loud body prayer to remind yourself of God's friendship, God's steadfastness, and God's availability. It may encourage you to reflect on all the ways God has guided and sustained you. Throw your body and your voice into this prayer as you follow the instructions by Joyce Rupp:

> Stand with arms outstretched and eyes wide open. Speak aloud all the names and qualities of God that come to your mind and heart. Let this be a litany of praise and thanksgiving for the gift of God in your life. When your litany is completed, fold your hands across your heart and bow your head in honor and reverence.[14]

A Second Spiritual Practice of Finding: All Will Be Well

Anchoress and mystic Julian of Norwich (1342–1416) is well known for having said, "All will be well and all will be well and every kind of thing shall be well."[15] For a week, repeat this affirmation each morning.

This may help you to take the long view and to trust the end of the story.

A Third Spiritual Practice of Finding:
End the Day with Thanks

Every night before I go to bed, I ask myself two questions that call me back to the practice of finding God's mercies:

What have been my sources of grace this day?
For what do I give thanks?

I've been doing this for years, and it makes a huge difference in how I regard my life. And I've become less of a whiner. Even on days when I've been in pain or in deep despair, these two questions have called me back to the big picture of finding grace and living in thanksgiving.

Questions to Ponder

Let God in

֍ How are you making space for God in your life? Is there anything you'd like to change?

- Is God your friend? If so, what are the fruits of that friendship for you?
- How is the Holy Spirit moving in your life right now? Is the Spirit nudging or guiding or getting your attention in any particular way?

Trust God more

- In the years of your life so far, what has led you to trust God more?
- What particular obstacles lie in your way of trusting God right now?
- How would you like to deepen your trust in God? How might that happen?

Embrace God's mercies

- How are you clothing yourself with God's mercies?
- How have they empowered and restored you?
- How might you become more conscious of God's mercies each day?

Chapter Five

Unearthing Blessing and Finding the Holy in Unexpected Places

As a church service ends, those sent out into the world receive a blessing or a benediction. The word "benediction" is from the Latin verb *benedicere*, which means to speak (*dicere*) good (*bene*) things about. Author and preacher Barbara Brown Taylor says, "To pronounce a blessing on something is to see it from the divine perspective."[1] When we bless something, we confer goodness on it and declare it holy.

Blessing is not something foreign to us, but something we do all the time. We bless our food before we eat. We bless ourselves and each other before we go to bed. We bless our prayer shawls. We bless our babies when we baptize them. We bless our couples when we marry them. We bless our dead when we bury them. The goal is to be more intentional in our blessing until we just start doing it all the time. Waiting for a train to go by? Try blessing the folks sitting in the cars behind you. Waiting for your turn at the dentist's office? Look around the waiting room and bless the others who are waiting with you. Standing in line at the grocery store? Bless that harried young mother with those three screaming children and throw in an extra blessing for the cashier who didn't get her lunch break.

We all have the power to bless. We all have the voice to pronounce something good. When we do, we see the world as God sees it. Here are several ways to embrace our own belovedness and to see the belovedness in others.

Accept the blessing of your belovedness

One of the greatest gifts in my life is that my father loved me to pieces. As a child, my whole life opened positively in front of me because of this simple fact. I was blessed, not cursed. This has shaped me and grounded me for decades. Because I realized early on that I was loved by my dad no matter what, a wealth of things became possible.

One of my colleagues in ministry works in the Wisconsin prison system. She says that so many of the young men she sees every week have never been treated kindly, have never been encouraged in any way, have never received love. They have been cursed, not blessed, and the consequences have been disastrous for them and for our society.

Each of us possesses a deep yearning to be loved and blessed, no matter what age we are. We ache to be affirmed, to be encouraged, to be told over and over that despite our stumblings and our failings, we are worthwhile.

One of my favorite scriptures in the Bible is from the Gospel of Mark 1:1–11, a passage that tells the story of Jesus being baptized by John in the Jordan. Just as he's coming up out of the water, he sees the heavens opening and the Spirit descending on him like a dove. A voice coming from heaven proclaims, "You are my Child, the Beloved; with you I am well pleased."² God is talking to God's child, Jesus, but of course this message is meant for every single one of us as well.

What does it mean for each one of us to be God's beloved? And how do we accept the blessing of our belovedness?

Our competitive and seductive culture is constantly trying to disparage our belovedness, making it difficult for us to believe the message. We hear merciless voices say: *Be rich. Be thin. Be beautiful. Be smart. Be popular. Be sexy. Be daring.* These voices tell us that we'll never measure up. Channel-surfing on cable TV the other day, I was appalled to see pictures of naked girls with certain crucial areas of their anatomies blocked out, the rest of their bodies marked up for plastic surgery, in a reality show I didn't know existed. In this particular episode, some seriously misled mother proudly scheduled surgery for her two young daughters. One daughter was to receive breast enhancement, and the other, breast reduction. Fascinated and horrified at the same time, I couldn't change channels. This mother, who could have been so influential in encouraging her daughters to feel loved and safe and comfortable in their bodies, chose to say instead, "You will never be good enough unless you conform to cultural expectations." In contrast, we hear God say to us, "You are my beloved child: with you I am well pleased."

The negative voices all around us are loud, insistent, and demanding. They make it hard for us to believe that we'll ever measure up, and we learn to despise ourselves. Often the greatest challenge to God's belovedness is our own self-rejection. When we fail, when we make mistakes, we say, "I'm pathetic. I'm stupid. I knew I couldn't do it right. I should never have tried. Nobody could possibly love me the way I am." When we succeed, we undermine ourselves in the same graceless way: "Yes, I did okay, but it must have been an accident. And now things are worse than ever. I managed to jump through that hoop, but now I'll have to jump through hoops until I die. I'll have to prove myself over and over again."

Still, the divine message is loud and clear: "You are my beloved child; with you I am well pleased." We all possess a vast capacity to wallow in self-rejection, reciting ways in which we will never, ever make the grade. But what if we started to live out of our beloved-ness rather than our fear? How would we receive and accept this blessing of belovedness again and again? Theologian Henri Nouwen offers a suggestion:

> Prayer then is listening to that voice—to the One who calls you the Beloved. It is to constantly go back to the truth of who we are and claim it for ourselves. I'm not what I do. I'm not what people say about me. I'm not what I have. . . . My life is rooted in my spiritual identity. Whatever we do, we have to go back regularly to that place of core identity.[3]

As with any spiritual discipline, claiming our belovedness takes practice. We will continue to sabotage ourselves with self-rejection, but we must keep calling ourselves back to belovedness again and again by listening to our voices of love. These are the voices we must vow to take seriously and to live by, the voices coming from friends and family members and neighbors and colleagues who believe in us and keep us safe. These are the benevolent, empowering voices, the voices that elevate our self-esteem and assure us that we are worthy. The strongest voice of love is God's voice, the voice of our Friend, the voice that says, "You are my beloved."

A second way in which we accept the blessing of our belovedness is to bask in God's love and then to pass that love on—by intentionally blessing others. We can bless others in a variety of ways, and one of those ways is prayer. The other day I received a lovely note from one of the people who comes to me for spiritual direction. She thanked me for my spiritual guidance, but then she made a special point to also thank me for my prayer. At the end of each hour-long session with a client, we both pause and bow our heads, and I offer up a prayer. In that prayer, I always try to gather up the issues that have made themselves known. I thank God for this person's gifts. I ask God to heal what needs to be healed. I pray that this person may know that they are held lavishly in the love of God. Once in a while, after the "Amen," I look up to see that the one who has been prayed over is weeping. It is at that moment that I know that this is the essence of my work. This blessing is the most important part. If I had no other skills but knew only how to pray and to bless, that would be enough.

We can also intentionally bless others by offering a hug, or by stopping and listening, or by offering encouragement. We bless people when we affirm their call or purpose or admire their creativity. We bless people by sincerely complimenting them or by dropping them a note of thanks and praise. There are all kinds of ways to bless other people by believing in them and pronouncing them good.

A third way in which we can accept the blessing of our belovedness is by intentionally blessing our enemy. This might be an advanced blessing course, not Blessing 101 but Blessing 401, and it is a true test of our spiritual confidence. As we give this some thought, we ask ourselves from whom we're withholding blessing and whom we've refused to bless. This is the most demanding spiritual work there is.

But when we bless our enemy, there may be a blessing within a blessing: we may discover our own shadow. An enemy is sometimes (though not always) an enemy because that person reminds us of something we struggle with or despise in ourselves. Folks in twelve-step programs say, "If you spot it, you got it."[4] In other words, that enemy may represent to us our shadow. In Jungian psychology, the shadow is "a part of the unconscious mind consisting of repressed weaknesses, shortcomings, and instincts."[5] If we bless our enemy, it may be that we learn to bless that spurned and contemptible part of ourselves. Luke 6:41 asks, "Why do you see the speck in your neighbor's eye, but do not notice the log in your own eye?" When we ask ourselves who our enemy is, we list all the things about him or her that drive us crazy. But how many of those things are present in our own personality? Does this enemy come bearing a gift of empathy or insight? When we begin to consider blessing our enemy, it may help us feel freer and lighter, and even a bit more self-forgiving as well.

Suspend judgment and look for the blessing

Life can be confounding, bewildering, enigmatic. Blessings can be hidden. When we take time to pay attention and to unearth blessing—when we practice finding—we enter into some deep excavation work that may require our asking a simple question: "Where is the blessing here?" Physician Rachel Naomi Remen says, "[T]he wisdom lies in engaging the life you have been given as fully and courageously as possible and not letting go until you find the unknown blessing that is in everything."[6] Sometimes it takes deliberateness and perseverance to discover those blessings. In 2017 my husband fell off a tall ladder, losing half an inch of length in his right leg and shattering his heel in seven places. For the next four months, he couldn't walk or drive. Though his healing was uppermost in my mind and heart, I was exhausted by all the extra chores and felt sorry for myself for quite a while. But then I began to discover something: I was becoming more capable. I was taking on unexpected responsibility, learning new skills, becoming more confident. And there was a second unexpected blessing: the support of family and friends who provided gratifying visits and parties, phone calls, rides, favorite books, meals, baked goods, and encouraging cards. This stream of blessings was a steady grace that kept us afloat.

Bless the limitations—even your own

Buddhist monk and meditation teacher Jack Kornfield relates a remarkable story about renowned violinist Itzhak Perlman blessing limitations—right in the middle of a performance:

> Perlman was stricken with polio as a child; he has braces on both his legs and walks with two crutches. He crosses the stage slowly, yet majestically, until he reaches his chair. Then he sits down, lowers his crutches to the floor, undoes the clasps on his legs, bends down and picks up the violin, puts it under his chin, nods to the conductor, and proceeds to play.
>
> But one time at a concert at Avery Fisher Hall at Lincoln Center in New York City, something went

wrong. In the middle of the concert, one of the strings on his violin broke. You could hear it snap—it went off like a gunshot. There was no mistaking what that sound meant: he would not be able to play the piece as it was written on his violin. People who were there wondered whether he'd have to put on the braces and go backstage—to find another violin or another string. But he didn't. Instead, he waited a moment, closed his eyes, and then signaled for the conductor to begin again. The orchestra began, and Perlman played on only three strings, modulating the piece in his head and adapting it to use the remaining strings with passion, steadiness, and remarkable purity.

When he finished, an awed silence filled the room. Then people stood and applause rose from every corner of the auditorium, bravos and cheering. Perlman smiled, wiped the sweat from his brow, raised his bow to quiet the audience, and then he said—not boastfully, but in a quiet, pensive, reverent tone—"You know, sometimes your task in life is to find out how much music you can still make with what you have left."[7]

How much music can we still make with what we have left? This is what blessing our limitations is all about. Each one of us is eventually aware of limitations, restraints brought on by disability, illness, or lack of opportunity. It can be grievously hard to live with limitations, but sometimes they expand our reach and embolden us to make a new kind of music:

- Limitations inspire us to be grateful for what is.
- Limitations encourage us to strengthen what remains.[8]
- Limitations allow us to understand suffering.
- Limitations provide us relief or freedom from doing something for which we were not suited.
- Limitations teach us to depend upon the gifts of others.

One powerfully self-aware way in which we can bless our limitations is by blessing our mistakes, because our errors and our sins open the door to a wealth of self-knowledge. This is a humbling and occasionally humiliating path to wisdom, but it definitely gets us there. As Wayne Muller says, "When Catholics enter the confessional they begin by saying, 'Bless me, for I have sinned.' Not 'judge me, punish me, berate me,' but 'bless me.' A sin, then, is an invitation to bless and be blessed."[9] If we stop and ponder our mistakes instead of blindly charging on in denial, we will grow and learn and be blessed.

Turn blessing into a daily practice

How we begin a day often sets the tone for the rest of it. One of the most intimate and tender parts of my day is the morning prayer that my husband, John, and I share at the breakfast table as we bless the world, our children, ourselves, and each other. This morning ritual helps me to feel grounded and grateful each day. These acts of blessing can take many different forms. Author Norman Cousins tells us about the morning ritual of the late cellist Pablo Casals:

> I met [Pablo Casals] for the first time at his home in Puerto Rico just a few weeks before his ninetieth birthday. I was fascinated by his daily routine. About 8 A.M. his lovely young wife Marta would help him to start the day. His various infirmities made it difficult for him to dress himself. Judging from his difficulty in walking and from the way he held his arms, I guessed he was suffering from rheumatoid arthritis. His emphysema was evident in his labored breathing. . . . He was badly stooped. His head was pitched forward and he walked with a shuffle. His hands were swollen and his fingers were clenched.
>
> Even before going to the breakfast table, Don Pablo went to the piano—which, I learned, was a daily ritual. . . .

I was not prepared for the miracle that was about to happen. The fingers slowly unlocked and reached toward the keys like the buds of a plant toward the sunlight. His back straightened. He seemed to breathe more freely. Now his fingers settled on the keys. Then came the opening bars of Bach's *Wohltemperiertes Klavier*, played with great sensitivity and control. . . . He hummed as he played, then said that Bach spoke to him here—and he placed his hand over his heart.

Then he plunged into a Brahms concerto and his fingers, now agile and powerful, raced across the keyboard with dazzling speed. His entire body seemed fused with the music; it was no longer stiff and shrunken but supple and graceful and completely freed of its arthritic coils.[10]

This unusual morning ritual, which could be called a blessing, might provide us with fresh ideas on how to begin our own days.

At day's end, we return to blessing. I find bedtime to be a particularly fruitful time to review the events of the day. Rather than painfully reliving those scenarios that were especially negative or vulnerable, I try touching them with blessing. This practice has enriched my life and my faith, and I recommend it to you. When we slowly surround those difficult interactions with warmth and light, we may find some peace of heart.

Practices and Ponderings

A First Spiritual Practice of Finding:
Bless a Living Thing and Discover Its Essence

It is thrilling when we bless a flower or a bird or an animal, and by doing so we notice its unique characteristics, behavior, and beauty. When we practice blessing, we comprehend our connectedness and kinship to that living thing. The next time you take a walk, see what you behold and scatter some blessings.

A Second Spiritual Practice of Finding:
Bless Your Calendar

You can choose to do this daily, weekly, or monthly in your datebook or on your phone. Observe how blessing—making holy—your calendar or your daily schedule affects the tenor of your activities, meetings, and commitments.

A Third Spiritual Practice of Finding:
Bless Your Obstacles

When we bless our obstacles, we find the holy in unexpected places. Author Christina Baldwin says, "When you hit an obstacle, write out everything good it is offering you. Bless it. Love it. Send it light."[11] Take a moment to think about this, because it's a counter-intuitive approach. What good things are your obstacles offering you right now?

A Fourth Spiritual Practice of Finding:
Bless Your Mortality

Mortality might be considered a paradoxical blessing, limiting and expansive at the same time. Emily Dickinson wrote, "That it will never come again / is what makes life so sweet."[12] There is usually a moment of reckoning in late middle age when we comprehend that there are more years behind us than out in front of us. Wherever you are in life, bless your mortality and cherish your remaining years.

Questions to Ponder

Accept the blessing of your belovedness

§ How have you experienced belovedness in your life? How has this empowered you?

§ What does thinking of yourself as being God's beloved allow? How might you begin to embrace this as your core identity?

§ How have you sabotaged or rejected your belovedness?

§ What does your heart feel like when you are asked to bless an enemy? How can your heart be softened?

Suspend judgment and look for the blessing

§ Where have you unearthed blessing and found the holy during your life? Where are you finding it right now?

§ Who or what is difficult for you to bless? Can you bring this to your prayer?

§ What blessing has arisen out of adversity?

Bless the limitations—even your own

§ During your life so far, what have been your limitations? What have you learned from them? How does it feel to bless them?

- ﹩ How does it feel to bless others' limitations?
- ﹩ How might you grow from blessing your mistakes and your sins? How might God be extending an invitation here?

Turn blessing into a daily practice

- ﹩ What daily practice of blessing might be most helpful to you?
- ﹩ How could you bless the beginning or end of your days?
- ﹩ How could you bless your food when you eat?
- ﹩ How could you truly bless yourself?

CHAPTER SIX

Owning Yourself and Finding
What Shapes Your Inimitable Being

Assume-toi. Own yourself. It's a French expression that entrances and empowers with its directive. Assume yourself. Own yourself. This admonition bids me to stand taller, to navigate my life more freely, to take on the world with confidence and power. *Assume-toi* means don't underestimate yourself, don't doubt yourself, but live into your fullness. Own all of yourself.

Spiritual teacher and author Marianne Williamson once said, "There's nothing enlightened about shrinking so that other people won't feel insecure around you. We are all meant to shine."[1] *Assume-toi* echoes that and encourages each of us to shine brightly. In one of her precious *anytime prayers* Madeleine L'Engle paints a picture of a grandfather showing his grandchildren the wonders of God's creation—moon, planets, and stars—through the eye of a telescope. Through the voice of one of the children, L'Engle completes her piece: "'See,' Grandfather said, 'what wonders God has made!' And then he hugged each one of us and said, 'And you are wondrous too!'"[2]

Here are several suggestions that I hope will help you to fully own your wondrous self.

Remember those who encouraged you

When I was three, my mom went back to work, and my grandma became my babysitter. She doted on me, but that spoiling had only positive effects. I was secure in her love, and I was empowered by it. My father, as I've already mentioned, also loved me unconditionally and was deeply nurturing. As a child, I had a life that was filled with possibility because I was safely loved by these two people.

When I was twelve, my world history teacher taught me about the contributions of ancient civilizations as surveyed in the epic work of Will and Ariel Durant. More importantly, she believed in me and trusted my potential. Encouragement from my father, his mother, and my world history teacher changed my life. As the Persian poet Rumi says, "Your lamp was lit from another lamp. / All God wants is your gratitude for that."[3]

To be formed well, we have to have at least one person who believes in us. This isn't about narcissism, but about a positive sense of self-worth. At different points in our lives, it's helpful to pause and remember the people who most believed in us when we were children and to consider what that meant for our future.

We are also shaped and formed by those who launched us, who urged us on with a loving push. Remember when you first rode a bicycle and had to have someone hold you steady and then push you off? A loving push[4] can change everything. My loving push came from author Julia Cameron in *The Artist's Way*. I would never have had the tools or the courage to get my first book published had I not read that book and adopted the practices it suggested. Cameron taught me to trust my own gifts and God's companionship on my creative path.

When we want to own ourselves fully, it's necessary for us to have an outlet for our gifts, an environment in which our talents are recognized and allowed to flourish. During what I have come to call the Siege of 2017, the four months during which my husband couldn't walk, he and I frequently visited the cast room of the orthopedic department in one of Milwaukee's big hospitals. The cast technician who unbound my husband's shattered foot and then bandaged it up again was a young man whom I shall call Tariq, who emigrated from Syria in 2014. This lowly cast tech was actually an orthopedic doctor from Syria who had graduated from medical school and had completed two years of orthopedic residency. Tariq was lonely in Milwaukee, separated from his fiancée and his parents in Syria, and in significant despair over his future in the current political climate. During these four months, I happened to catch a story on NPR that reminded me once again of the necessity of a supportive environment in which to express one's gifts. The story was about Dr. Carmen Bachmann, who decided to make it her mission to encourage refugee academics and to create a supportive environment for them.[5]

Dr. Carmen Bachmann is a dynamic young woman who is a professor of tax and finance at Leipzig University. In 2016, over one million refugees arrived in Germany, six thousand of them settling in Leipzig alone. Dr. Bachmann was aware that many German citizens were volunteering to collect furniture or clothing, but as a full professor, she decided she could do more. She learned that there were refugees with advanced degrees living in the temporary camps, and she decided this is where she could make a difference. "I know the special needs for people with an academic background," Dr. Bachmann says, "and this is what I can contribute. I thought, 'If they wait one year and they stop researching and stop studying, it's a big loss. It's a loss for the people who lost their knowledge. It's a loss for society.'"

Dr. Bachmann's first step was to help these academics find employment, so she called the Federal Employment Agency in Leipzig and discovered that most of the job listings were for unskilled laborers. Undaunted, she was determined to create a website that would make it possible for refugee scientists to connect with German scientists. These connections might lead to employment or collaboration or an invitation to a seminar or access to research journals. Most of all, the website could help isolated refugee academics remain involved and engaged. Dr. Bachmann and one of her grad students worked day and night to get the new website, Chance-for-Science, up and running; she also gave interview after interview. German media were buzzing, universities were excited, but nothing happened. Not one refugee signed up.

Once again, Dr. Bachmann remained unfazed. She decided she would just have to go to the refugees—in person. She remembered that when she had been a teenager and a single mother living on welfare, it was a former high school teacher who encouraged her, believed in her potential, and saved her life. Dr. Bachmann recalled that the teacher visited her almost every other week and brought her books. "We made a walk in the park with my child, and we just talked," she explained. "This somehow kept me alive— that I could talk about these books with someone."

Spurred on by this memory, Dr. Bachmann was determined to visit the refugees. So she went to a large refugee camp in Leipzig, where she was shocked by the crowded conditions, the small beds, the lack of privacy. She really didn't know what to do, so she just started handing out fliers and walking around, saying, "Hello, is there anyone speaking English or speaking German? I am Carmen from the University." At first the refugees were hesitant, not knowing what to make of this determined young woman. But finally they began to approach her one by one, saying, "I have nothing. But I have my diploma." Most of the academics had their diplomas with them, these precious pieces of paper that represented their passion, their vision, their work. They had fled with only their prized possessions, and diplomas were among them. One Syrian engineer said, "I feel like nothing here. In Syria I was a professor, and I come here—I can do much more than sitting around."

Today, more than five hundred people have registered on Dr. Bachmann's website, both refugees and German academics. Because Dr. Bachmann remembered being encouraged by one of her teachers, she decided to pass on this encouragement to refugee academics by never giving up on them.

Inspired by Dr. Bachmann's example, my husband and I nurtured and encouraged the kind young Syrian doctor every time we visited the cast room. We made a special effort to tell him that we were grateful for the good care he provided, that he mattered in our lives, and that we trusted he would eventually have a bright future. On one of our last visits to the hospital, I took him home-baked pastries that were similar to those he savored in Syria.

Affirm the truths that have set you free

As a parent in the late 1980s, I experienced a significant turning point. My two children were young, my husband and I were trying to balance our careers and run a household, and I was depleted and perplexed. Did everyone but me know how to make life run smoothly?

Fueled by high anxiety, I was trying to do everything perfectly. Each meal had to be superb, each birthday present just right, each enrichment activity successfully assessed and faultlessly chosen. If I could carry out each responsibility flawlessly, I thought, I'd be the perfect parent. Instead, I was an anxious, over-achieving, and way-too-serious parent.

Exhausted, I attended a parenting class. A simple sentence from the instructor struck home: "What your children will remember is your state of mind." This truth set me on a whole new path. My learning to lighten up, to let go, and to embrace "good enough" parenting improved our lives considerably. I lowered my standards and became happier, more confident— and a better parent!

My children are grown now, but I still remember that instructor's message. Now I turn that statement into a discernment question and use it as a plumb line: *What is my state of mind right now?* That teacher offered me a truth that has set me free.

We can also affirm our truths by recalling what gives us perspective. I've come across a number of spiritual tools that consistently offer me that gift. Several of the tools are short quotations that I turn to again and again:

I've seen trouble and this ain't it.

—Dave Wilson (my father)

Go through the door that's open.

—Toinette Lippe[6]

If you want a chicken to be a duck, and a duck to be a chicken, you will suffer.

—Ajahn Chah[7]

The wave is not the sea.

—Mark Nepo[8]

Be yourself; everyone else is already taken.

—Oscar Wilde[9]

And I consistently rely on this discernment meditation called "Reflecting on Difficulty" by Jack Kornfield:

> How have I treated this difficulty so far?
> How have I suffered by my own
> response and reaction to it?
> What does this problem ask me to let go of?
> What suffering is unavoidable, is my measure to
> accept?
> What great lesson might it be able to teach me?
> What is the gold, the value, hidden in this
> situation?[10]

Another discovery I've made: perspective is gained by getting out of town. Going away sets me free from the familiar, releasing me from habitual responses and solutions, as it generates fresh perspective and new thinking.

When I need a little inspiration for my musings, I do a life review to affirm my own truths. I ask what the decades have taught me and what I'm proud of having discovered and learned. And when I want to think about the big picture, I'm helped by definitions of wisdom, like this one by Martin Copenhaver:

Philosophers, theologians, and social scientists have all found wisdom notoriously difficult to define. In part, this is because wisdom is more than a single attribute. It is more like a cluster of attributes, including a cleareyed view of human behavior, coupled with keen self-understanding; a certain tolerance for ambiguity and what might be called the messiness of life; emotional resiliency; an ability to think clearly in a circumstance of conflict or stress; a tendency to approach a crisis as an intriguing puzzle to be solved; an inclination to forgive and move on; humility enough to know that it is not all about you; a gift for seeing how smaller facts fit in within a larger picture; a mix of empathy and detachment; a knack for learning from lifetime experiences; a way of suspending judgment long enough to achieve greater clarity; an ability to act coupled with a willingness to embrace judicious inaction.[11]

Own your essence and your strengths

Own your passion

Assume-toi. Own yourself. Own all of yourself—your essence, "the basic, real, and invariable nature"[12] of you. And your passion. Those two things go hand in hand.

Sometimes when we start by understanding what we're passionate about—what makes us leap out of bed in the morning and keeps us up late at night, what makes us lose track of time—that reflects back to us our essence.

"What do you love so much that you lose track of time when you're doing it?" an instructor asked in a class I recently took called "Crossroads and Callings." I listed three things: integrating ideas and concepts into an understandable whole, sitting and listening to people who are trying to make sense of their lives, and designing and making jewelry. I'm passionate about all of these things, and I have no idea what time it is while I'm doing them.

The word "passion" can be divided up into PASS—I—ON.[13] (Isn't that fun?) What excites you the most? What do you love doing? How can you pass it on or share it with others?

Own your compassion

The English word "compassion" is from the Latin *com*, meaning "with," and *passio*, meaning "suffering." It's important to understand how you express compassion in your life, as well as how you have aligned yourself with those who suffer. Are you isolating yourself from those who suffer? Are you holding yourself at a distance? Noticing who is suffering and then contributing to the alleviation of that suffering is marvelously satisfying and deepens connection with all of humanity.

When I was a child, my mother and father committed themselves to the disabled members of our congregation, many of whom were in wheelchairs and socially isolated. My parents taught me to look for and to pay attention to those who were left out. As that ministry grew, I accompanied my mom and dad on outings and picnics they had planned. Later, when I was a teenager, I worked for a number of summers as a volunteer at United Cerebral Palsy of Columbus, Ohio. Inspired by my joy in this work and all that I received in return, I became a speech pathology major in college.

Own the wisdom of your body

Sit down. Sit *with* your body. And reminisce for a while. Savor your body and soak in the majesty of it, which is a part of God's good and wondrous creation. Recall what you've been through together over the years. What has your body taught you about being human? How has your body been faithfully there for you? How has your body participated in your healing? What joys and delights have you shared? How have these deepened your spirit? What trials and limitations have you shared? How have these deepened your spirit? Thank this intimate friend with an affirmation from Psalm 139 in the Bible: "I am fearfully and wonderfully made; I am fearfully and wonderfully made."

Own your courage

Eleanor Roosevelt, born in 1884, a woman before her time, eventually became known as "First Lady of the World" for her outspokenness and her activism against racism and on behalf of human rights. If it was necessary, she did not hesitate to disagree with her husband, President Franklin Delano Roosevelt. Over and over again, I have looked to Eleanor Roosevelt to give me courage to face my fears and have been empowered by this well-known quotation:

> You gain strength, courage, and confidence by every experience in which you really stop to look fear in the face.
>
> You are able to say to yourself, "I lived through this horror. I can take the next thing that comes along."

The danger lies in refusing to face the fear, in not daring to come to grips with it. . . . *You must do the thing you think you cannot do.*[14]

At a recent conference, I heard the Rev. Traci Blackmon tell a sweet story of courage—out of the mouth of babes. On her first Easter Sunday at her congregation, she had the children prepare little Easter speeches. One ten-year-old boy refused to present his speech and began to cry in fear. But later he changed his mind and burst forth loudly with the words he had prepared. Rev. Blackmon asked the child, "What happened? How did you overcome your fear to finally do it?" The little boy replied, "I didn't. I just did it afraid."

The word "courage" is related to the French word for "heart," *coeur*, and the Latin word for "heart," *cuer*. Impelled to act in the way our hearts say is right, we frequently suffer challenging trade-offs, penalties, and ostracism. Exhibiting this kind of steadfastness, fearlessness, and courage is not for the weak of heart.

Psychologist Harriet Lerner lists six ways in which we exhibit courage:

- There is courage in taking action.
- There is courage in speaking.
- There is courage in questioning.
- There is courage in pure listening.

· There is courage in thinking for ourselves.
· There is courage in being accountable.[15]

It helps me to have this list as I look over my life and review the times and places in which I dared to act courageously as well as those in which I did not. Reminding us that "life shrinks or expands in proportion to one's courage," diarist Anaïs Nin inspires us to reflect on how courage has reshaped and enlarged our lives.[16] Perhaps you're exhibiting great courage at this moment, and like the little boy at church, you haven't claimed your courage, but are going ahead anyway—and are just *doing it afraid*.

Own your special gift to the world

For most of us, there is an underlying role we play all our lives, whether in our paid work or our volunteer work. It is just who we are. My husband, who is a physician, knows that he is most of all a teacher. A colleague of mine, who is a pastor, identifies herself as a healer.

My friend Anne, who grew up as the oldest of five, experiences her underlying role as scout. Sent off to primary school, she felt the burden of being her guarded and anxious family's representative in the world, with the duty to report back on how things worked "out there." At each successive stage, the scope of that task grew—through graduate school, professional life, and travel around the globe. It became her interpretive role and her calling to report back to students, colleagues, family, and friends on the requirements, pitfalls, and possibilities of an intrepid and expansive life.

There are various names for your special gift to the world. Author and spiritual guide Marjory Zoet Bankson calls it *charism*, which she describes this way:

> *Charism* is an archaic word that describes the unique gift of who we are, the character or soul we are born with. The Greek root of the word is "gift of God's grace." *Charism* is not earned or schooled; it is given to be explored and developed, not harnessed and driven for success. *Charism* is commonly thought to be a special gift, something that certain people have for drawing others to them. We sometimes speak of a charismatic leader or charismatic personality, but in truth, we each have a *charism*, a gift we are called to bear in the world. It defines who we are and how we relate to others. [17]

As I consider my *charism*—or, as I think of it, my underlying role—as a provider of hospitality, I find that these are some of the gifts I bear in the world:

- welcoming people to share a meal at our table
- providing safety and confidentiality for those who come to me for spiritual direction
- offering a peaceful and nurturing environment to those who attend my retreats
- listening to people's stories and offering them encouragement for who they are

As we begin to think about our own *charism*, some of us may be able name it immediately, while others may need some time. But most of us, once we name our *charism*, can describe how this special gift has brought us joy and allowed us to realize our life's purpose.

Assume-toi. Own yourself. When I do this, I am filled with confidence as well as reverence—when I pause to perform the holy task of owning myself and when I stop to absorb what it means. Fearfully and wonderfully made, we are multifaceted biological miracles—empowered and made strong as we recall all the parts of our dazzling, shining, and capable selves. The practice of finding helps us to understand and embrace the abundant and unique creation that is each one of us: our essence, our wholeness, every aspect of our inimitable and wondrous being.

Practices and Ponderings

A First Spiritual Practice of Finding:
Draw Your Essence

Get out a piece of paper and something to draw with. Think of a metaphor that represents your essence. Remembering that you are fearfully and wonderfully made, make a drawing, a simple drawing of that image or metaphor.

A Second Spiritual Practice of Finding:
Compose a Prayer of Thanksgiving about Yourself

Assume-toi. The practice of finding compels us to reflect with awe on all the amazing, astounding aspects of ourselves. Each of us is one of a kind among the approximately seven billion people on earth right now. There has been no other like you before you were born, and there will be no one like you after you die. Own yourself. Own all of yourself. Compose a prayer of thanksgiving about yourself and your unique gifts that you are grateful to have and to share.

A Third Spiritual Practice of Finding:
Count Your Contributions

At the end of the day, count your blessings *and* your contributions. Try this for a week and see if you're feeling more capable. Sheryl Sandberg, COO of Facebook, says, "Contributions are active: they build our confidence by reminding us that we can make a difference."[18]

Questions to Ponder

Remember those who encouraged you

- ✦ Whom do you most credit for having shaped you into the person you are today?
- ✦ Who gave you confidence?
- ✦ Who or what created an environment in which your gifts could be expressed?

Affirm the truths that have set you free

- ✦ What are the sayings that you live by?
- ✦ What bits of your own hard-earned wisdom would be most helpful for a young person to internalize and to know?

Own your essence and your strengths

- § How do you name your strengths? How do others name them?
- § How do you view yourself as a unique part of God's creation?
- § Do you struggle to own all of yourself? Where is God in this?
- § How do you own yourself? How do you own all of yourself?

Chapter Seven

Overcoming Hindrances to Gratitude and Finding Thankfulness Once Again

Sometimes the practice of finding comes very easily. Sometimes it doesn't. Occasionally we encounter impediments that make gratitude nearly impossible. We sabotage ourselves as we relentlessly compare ourselves with others, as we become obsessed with accumulating more, as we remain trapped in insecurity and ruled by fear, or as we feel there will never be *enough*. Blinded to gratitude, we become frightfully self-absorbed, but the good news is that with a little self-awareness we can be back on a positive, life-giving path.

Here are several ways to reach that path.

Release the temptation to compare

The other night after dinner I felt grumpy and rattled, disgruntled and upset. My equilibrium had been disturbed by all the things I wanted and couldn't have. My husband and I had been invited by friends to their lavishly appointed home, and I was overwhelmed by much that was elegant, exquisite, imported, and very, very expensive. As they say, comparison is the thief of happiness. Later that evening, when I walked into my suddenly outdated home, I was filled with dissatisfaction. Burdened with envy, I wanted every gorgeous piece of furniture, every wall covering, every window treatment, every piece of cookware that belonged to our friends—even though, a few hours earlier, I had delighted in my spacious and welcoming kitchen.

Now when I looked at my dining table, it seemed shabby, and my countertops worn. It took me a couple of days to settle down and stop obsessing, to exorcize that temptation to compare, and to gain a bit of perspective. Constantly wanting what we can't have and don't need wears us out and turns us into people who are incapable of thanksgiving. Comparisons get us nowhere.

There are two "Evil E's" that fuel our constant comparing: envy and entitlement. Envy can kill our spirit, taking gratitude, contentment, and peace of mind along with it. When we listen to it, envy tells us that we've lost perspective and that we're meddling, that we're minding someone else's business rather than our own. And envy, when we take a sharp look at it, almost always points to something deeper. It may indicate that we're not living up to our own expectations or that we're not being true to ourselves. When we experience envy, it's helpful to ask, What's the deeper meaning here?

The second Evil E is entitlement. In my book *Seven Spiritual Gifts of Waiting*, I wrote: "Entitlement defeats gratitude. Entitlement is a continual comparing, insisting on getting more than someone else. If we believe that we are getting less than we deserve, there is no way we will be content, let alone grateful."[1] Have you ever been on vacation in another country with Americans who travel to broaden their experience, yet continually complain if everything isn't exactly the convenient and efficient way it is at home? That's entitlement. The pushiness and arrogance of entitlement crowd out the practice of finding. It closes us down and can creep in and overtake us when we least expect it. When you find yourself thinking, "I deserve this" or "I deserve that," it's time to beware: a grateful heart is not an entitled heart.

Purge your preoccupation with More

We will never live in gratitude if we continue insisting on more. In her timeless classic *Gift from the Sea*,

Anne Morrow Lindbergh says, "One cannot collect all the beautiful shells on the beach. One can collect only a few, and they are more beautiful if they are few."[2] The times we feel we're driven to accumulate are times to stop, take some deep breaths, and reflect on the word "Enough." (Some might consider a brief but intentional breath prayer: Breathing in *Enough.* Breathing out *More.*) Try it and see what happens. Maybe you'll experience a little realignment. Maybe you'll feel gratitude for what is.

To purge our preoccupation with More is also to purge the fear of missing something. Young people refer to this with the acronym FOMS.[3]

When I need groceries, I find myself gravitating more and more to a small neighborhood store where the choices don't seduce and overwhelm me. For a while I was shopping at a brand new mega-mart the size of a football field. There were 108 kinds of barbecue sauce. (Yes, I counted them.) I would come home with seven bags of groceries and have to take a nap, exhausted from touring the aisles of wine, the block-long deli, the cheese room, and the artisan's bakery. Most of all, I was weary of my own insatiable need to try everything. My FOMS quotient is pretty high. Knowing this, I've discovered that I have more peace of heart if I intentionally limit my choices. But how many choices are enough?

The relentless call to More can be limited by looking and not buying. At first this can be painful, but eventually it's freeing. In talking about "sustainable contentment," teacher Catherine Ingram says, "You don't have to keep adding more and more to your life. In fact, it feels really good to want what you have, [and] to take care of it."[4]

Our well-being is enhanced not by addictive spending and over-accumulation, but by appreciating beauty. We might go to an art fair and focus on the artists' creativity, relishing that—without having to buy anything. Or we might go into a shop or a gallery and admire the color and texture and forms we see—without bringing anything home. This takes practice, but gratitude is made sweeter when we pay attention to beauty and understand what is enough. One woman I know shares her good taste by decorating virtual rooms on Pinterest. "It's fun and cost-free!" she says. Finding thankfulness once again can be helped along by "just looking."

Yet another acronym describes our preoccupation with More: FOMO—the Fear of Missing Out. Even though we know there's way too much information on social media for any human being to absorb, we still remain frantic that we won't know it all and won't be up to date.

A few years ago I opted out of Facebook. At first I experienced FOMO—I knew I'd miss all that connecting and up-to-the-minute information. But eventually I felt relieved by releasing a web of distraction and a tangle of gossip and intrigue. No longer did I worry about adding friends, ignoring friend requests, or unfriending. And the inevitable constant-contact questions—Is my social life up to par? Am I as attractive as I might be? Smart enough?—began to dissipate. Now I connect with family on Instagram, which is just right. The exchange of photos makes me feel connected but not overwhelmed. And I have more time to read books and have lunch with friends.

In decades to come, we'll encounter even more advanced and comprehensive forms of social media. That's why it's important to begin now, taking stock of what provides us with genuine and satisfying connection and how much information is healthy for us to absorb.

If we're sincere about releasing our preoccupation with More, we'll want to be aware of our own *hedonic adaptation*. This term refers to a psychological process by which we adapt to a "new normal" after the trauma of a negative event or the elation of a positive one. Hedonic adaptation allows us to heal from bad things and to eventually recover, to integrate even grievous changes into a new self-image. But hedonic adaptation can also be troubling, letting us forget the uniqueness and bliss of the good fortune that comes our way, allowing us to lapse into a seductive kind of entitlement that demands more and more. In other words, *you get used to what you get used to.* While hedonic adaptation can be helpful after injury or trauma, it can be dangerous and troubling after an event like winning the lottery. Become accustomed to five-star restaurants and thousand-dollar bottles of wine, and you've raised a high bar, risking numbness to sweet, small, daily pleasures.

The antidote to the kind of hedonic adaptation that results in too much privilege and entitlement? Insight and gratitude. To counteract a forgetting of life's true joys, we create a deliberate and consistent practice of finding. We haven't really experienced the good things until we've consciously noticed them. Noticing and actively being grateful go hand in hand. When we counteract hedonic adaptation, we release our preoccupation with More, relish simple joys—and live with contentment.

It's also easy to let the More of busyness crowd out gratitude. To protect gratitude, we need to say no to constant engagement and overcommitment. Relentless busyness deserves no kudos. More and more executives are discovering too much busyness impedes creativity and harms personal relationships. "Beware the barrenness of a busy life," Socrates said,[5] knowing that it can be desolate, without space for self-awareness and reflection. Of course, making money and keeping food on the table take a lot of energy, as do maintaining a home and raising children or taking care of elderly loved ones. Most of us are also involved in many activities requiring significant chunks of time. Busyness may be necessary simply because we bear many responsibilities, but it may also serve as a distraction from our soul's work. So, while we're scheduling our full days, we need to remember to offer gratitude some room on our calendar.

Rise above your insecurity

In our shyness, or our pain, or our woundedness, we are often insecure. A fierce impediment to gratitude, insecurity is a common malady. When we suffer from lack of self-esteem, we can become competitive or bitter. When we're insecure, situations are always all about us, preventing us from looking beyond ourselves or being grateful.

The more I sit with folks who come to me for spiritual direction, the more I understand how many of us are weighed down by heavy burdens for much of our lives. Even people who look as if they have it all together are often struggling and broken-hearted, working to be faithful, working to heal their wounds, working to get along with those they love. It reminds me that we're all in this mess together.

"Be kind, for everyone you meet is fighting a great battle" is a well-known saying attributed to Philo of Alexandria.[6] Look around. We're all insecure about one thing or another. Make an effort to rise above your insecurity. When that happens, you may be able to practice finding after all.

A few years ago on the Sunday after Thanksgiving, I was at the airport, having just dropped off our daughter, Katie, to board a flight back to her home in Boston. Our son had already left for his home in Minneapolis, my husband was at work, and I was feeling a little lonely and sorry for myself. It's hard to say good-bye. Would our children always live far away from us? (*Now* they live in San Francisco and Geneva, Switzerland!) Would we eventually be long-distance grandparents, forced to be content with holiday visits and mailed birthday packages, pre-arranged visits on Skype, occasional texts and WhatsApp chats? Would we always live so far apart, seeing each other only a few days a year? As I negotiated the airport traffic, I was firing up to be poor, poor, pitiful me. Imagining all the dismal scenarios I had sketched out, I became extremely anxious and fearful. Then, just as I pulled away from the airport, I noticed the license plate in front of me: B NT AFRD. "Oh, wow," I mumbled.

"License-plate theology at its best. 'Be not afraid.' This is what the angel said to the shepherds. This is just what I need right now." Fear shrinks us, preventing us from being who God created us to be. And fear definitely inhibits the practice of finding. When we release fear, it helps us rise above insecurity.

When we let go of fear and soften our hearts, we become more whole and more secure. When our hearts are hardened, filled with judgment, there is no room for light, openness, mercy, or forgiveness. Indeed, author Wayne Muller says, "Many spiritual traditions suggest that evil springs most swiftly from a heart that has been hardened."[7] If hardness of heart is weighing you down, begin the process of release. It may take a long time, but it will be worthwhile. When you become free and your heart begins to soften, you can practice finding once again.

When I meet with those who come to me for spiritual direction, I pray before our session, and most of the time I simply invoke the companionship of the Holy Spirit. If we meet during a particularly captivating liturgical season, I might refer to God's invitation during that particular time. For example, during this last season of Eastertide, I have been invariably praying this prayer: "God, help us to free ourselves from those things which entomb us and hold us down. Help us to roll those stones away and to welcome new birth and new life." Sometimes the person I'm meeting with describes forces that are restricting and entrapping. And of all those forces, regret is one of the most damaging and most potent.

If only. If only. If only. All of us have regrets about some of the ways we've acted or the way some things have turned out. We say wistfully, "If only." *If only I could forgive myself. If only I could forgive him or her. If only I could accept the horror or the injustice or the unfairness that has happened to me.* Finding healing might include journaling or making formal amends or perhaps seeking therapy. And it will surely benefit from the Serenity Prayer (which I discussed earlier), which helps us to discover something beyond regret:

> God, grant me the serenity to accept the things I
>   cannot change,
> Courage to change the things I can,
> And wisdom to know the difference.[8]

Moving beyond regret is one of the most restorative freedoms in the practice of finding.

Mark Twain once said, "I have been through some terrible things in my life, some of which actually happened."[9] His witty line makes an important point: worry does us no good and makes the practice of finding impossible. For me, worry has been a significant spiritual challenge. I used to worry so much that I manipulated those around me, constantly stirring up anxiety in others as well. I actually felt a great responsibility to worry. After all, someone had to do it! But over time I began to understand that worry bears no spiritual fruits. Worry never teaches us anything useful, nor can there be room for gratitude when worry takes center stage. When we worry, we lessen our trust in God and in our own good sense.

When worry causes us to distrust ourselves, we become crippled, constantly filled with uneasiness and fear. But when we believe we are capable, ethical, and resourceful, we meet a future that looks hopeful. That's how a writing teacher describes one of her students:

> One woman, now eighty, walks daily the two miles from home to our [writing] class and back, carrying only her backpack. . . . Headlines of rape and assault do not daunt her. After all, she has homesteaded the California desert; she has whitewater rafted on the Colorado River; she has driven the Alaskan highway in winter. She has left one husband because he drank; she has watched another one die. She has left a man she loved, at age seventy-two, because he was a gambler. Her eldest daughter she lost ten years ago to cancer. What has she left to fear? Confidently

she walks the streets, attends college, writes, paints, imagines her future.[10]

From such students we learn that when we overcome great challenges one by one, we discover a tried-and-true trust in ourselves that imbues us with confidence, allowing us to rise above our insecurity.

Practices and Ponderings

A First Spiritual Exercise of Finding:
How Many Eggs Can You Hold?

We are all occasionally crushed by an insidious busyness that dries up our souls and hinders the practice of finding. At these times, we are withered, weary, and overcome. In our "overwhelmedness," gratitude is nowhere to be found, but there's a wisdom-lesson here, as Wayne Muller explains:

> When we are children, we begin to find and collect "eggs"—people, ideas, dreams—that we like to hold in our hands. As our hands naturally grow larger over time, we are able to hold more eggs. Youth is a time of curiosity, gathering up and collecting more. The eggs slowly fill our hands. The more we grow,

the more eggs we can hold without fear of dropping them.

But at a certain point we stop growing, and our capacity to safely hold on to any more eggs stops growing with us. While different people have different-sized hands, and some can hold more or less than others, each of us has our own finite limit, beyond which, if we take on even just one more, things will start to fall, and whatever precious things we are carrying will invariably begin to break.

Once we have reached this moment of fullness, of satiation—of enough—we can only pick up a new egg if we carefully take at least one from the existing pile in our hands and gently put it down. We must let something go. This is no judgment about our ability, skillfulness, or power. It is simply the inevitable physics of a human life.[11]

How many eggs are you holding now? Can you name them? How many eggs *can* you hold? Right now, can you name one or more eggs that you need to put down?

A Second Spiritual Practice of Finding:
Overcoming Fear

Sufi poet Hafiz reminds us, "Fear is the cheapest room in the house. / I would like to see you living / In better conditions."[12] Though humorous, this quote may pierce our hearts. How may fear continue to be an obstacle to gratitude for you? How can you lessen your fear in order to practice finding again?

Questions to Ponder

Release the temptation to compare

- How have comparisons diminished you or caused trouble in your life? What kind of comparing lays you low?
- How have you battled envy or entitlement? How can you learn to identify these sooner when they crop up—and work to eliminate them from your life?

Purge your preoccupation with More

- What kind of preoccupation with More blocks your thankfulness? Too many choices, possessions, connections, privileges, responsibilities? Where do you get stuck?

§ Where in your life do you need to embrace the concept of Enough? Where is God's invitation here?

Rise above your insecurity

§ This section of the chapter explores fear, hardness of heart, regret, worry, and lack of self-trust as hindrances to gratitude. Which of these are culprits for you? How do they block your ability to be thankful?

§ What obstacles to gratitude are present in your life that may not have been mentioned in this chapter?

CHAPTER EIGHT

Valuing What You Have and Finding the Contentment of Enough

Finding and valuing what we already have lets us discover what is *enough* in our lives and all that sustains us. The practice of finding invites us to search our lives and notice what we've already secured in the way of possessions and relationships and achievements. Sue Monk Kidd tells a charming story about understanding that in a new way:

> One December when my daughter Ann was six, she tucked two gifts beneath the Christmas tree, one for her daddy, and the other for me. "What do you suppose they are?" I asked my husband. He shrugged, as puzzled as I.
>
> On Christmas morning I opened my gift to find a pair of slightly familiar-looking silver earrings. In her daddy's package was a navy tie with little tan ducks on it.

"Why, Ann," I exclaimed, genuinely amazed. "Where did you get these lovely gifts?"

"The cedar chest," she answered.

That's when I recognized the earrings as a pair I'd retired to the chest at least ten years before. The tie had been discarded long ago too. Ann had given us gifts we already possessed!

The incident caused me to consider how much my life was quietly caught in wanting, seeking, and acquisition. That trinity of all-American pursuits not only undermined my sense of what is enough, but seduced me into an artificial sense of discontent. Thanks to a six-year-old, I discovered the clean, simple wisdom of waking up to what I already have.[1]

The practice of finding provides an antidote to the commercial clamor of "more, more, more." That practice invites us to look closely for what is already ours: love, beauty, humor, friendship—perhaps a satisfying meal or an adoring pet. When you tuck yourself in for the night, one way to practice finding is simply to ask the question: What did I find today? *Practice finding. Practice finding.* It's a fine little mantra. Before I go to the mall or make a purchase online, I try to repeat it.

To increase your sense of contentment, try the finding practices below.

Reflect on happiness that money can't buy

Over the years as I've presented retreats on gratitude, I've asked participants to list their "Sources of Abundance." Over and over, their lists are filled with experiences of abundance that money can't buy:

- sharing laughter with a good friend
- sitting on the deck
- gardening
- watching a sunset
- enjoying the smell of pine
- listening to music
- spending time with my granddaughter
- praying
- enjoying the taste of fresh tomatoes and corn in July
- watching the orioles when they come to my birdfeeder

When we make these lists, they teach us to be continually amazed by what is around us now, already given, absolutely free. "Abundance can be had simply by consciously receiving what already has been given,"[2] a Sufi proverb says. It just takes a little looking and a little finding.

One of the masters of finding is Jesuit Anthony De Mello, who wrote this poem:

Riches

Husband: "I'm going to work hard, and someday we are going to be rich."
Wife: "We are already rich, dear, for we have each other. Someday maybe we'll have money."[3]

In an upstairs bedroom, I have a treasure drawer filled with thank-you notes and cherished cards and letters I've received over the years. This drawer is my go-to place to review messages of love and thanks—especially when I'm feeling unconfident, underappreciated, and generally blue. I practice finding by rereading these heartfelt notes. And as I do, my spirit is lifted, and I am filled with thankfulness. Once, the week after I preached a Mother's Day sermon, my friend Linda sent me the following note:

Holly, Greetings!
I <u>LOVED</u> your message on families Sunday—natural and chosen families. I'm grateful that you are part of my life and have showered me with grace and your extensive gifts. Thank you for being part of my chosen family!
Lovingly, Linda

As I read the note in Linda's lavish script on hand-made paper, it touched my heart deeply that she took the time to let me know in this extravagant way that she appreciated me. As you recall letters or cards of concern or written expressions of love or gratitude you've received, think about how these have been grace notes in your life.

Be glad when your needs are met

In the winter and spring of 2006 as my mother was dying, I flew to Columbus, Ohio, from Milwaukee, Wisconsin, every five to eight days. After several months of this, my husband and I brought my mom to hospice care in Wisconsin so I could be with her every day.

During those months, I depended on certain emotional and spiritual tools to keep me afloat. One of those practices was to ask each day: *Are my needs being met?* (food on the table, a listening ear, exercise, rest, etc.). Despite the constant challenges, most of the time I could honestly answer Yes. And that ability to answer affirmatively helped me to discover what was enough each day, like manna in the wilderness. Chinese philosopher Lao Tzu reminds me, "Be content with what you have; / rejoice in the way things are. /

When you realize there is nothing lacking, / the whole world belongs to you."[4]

During these months, putting pride aside, I learned to accept help—not my usual caregiving mode. One particularly disheartening spring day, I was exhausted and burdened by heavy sadness. As I drove around running errands, my cell phone rang: it was the hospice chaplain. "Holly, how are you doing?"

"I'm hanging in," I told him.

Then he asked, "Can we pray together?"

"What—now?"

"Yes, now. Can you pull over?"

"Sure. Wait a minute." I pulled the car to the shoulder of the road, and he began praying over that cell phone—praying for my strength, praying for my comfort, praying that I would have what I needed and that my mother would have what she needed. Tears rolled down my cheeks as my heart filled with gratitude for those much-needed words. And I received, bountifully. After the chaplain was finished, I said, "Thanks so much for remembering me and offering this prayer now." He had poured God's love right through me and satisfied the needs of my spirit. Because of him, I knew I could make it through another day.

One unusual way of remembering how your needs are met is by honoring a random act of kindness—and paying it forward. When I was a teenager, I got myself in a tight spot once. Not an experienced solo traveler, I found myself in a strange city with an invalid air ticket and no extra cash. As I stood at the ticket counter pleading with an airline agent, the man behind me simply handed me the money I needed and said, "Take the money, and do this for someone else someday." Thanksgiving over this generous, grace-filled gesture filled my eyes with tears. I have never forgotten it. And that stranger's unexpected response to my need has continued to influence my life. In gratitude, I have paid it forward. The great prophet of Yale University, William Sloane Coffin, writes, "[G]ratitude, not obedience, is the primary religious emotion. Duty calls only when gratitude fails to prompt."[5]

And I'll never forget a far bigger example of the needs of many being met with grace and resourcefulness. On Saturday morning, September 10, 2016, one day before the fifteenth anniversary of September 11, 2001, I stood in my kitchen bawling over a story that journalist Scott Simon reported on NPR. It was called "Rerouted Passengers Find Resilience in Gander," a story about met needs, random acts of kindness, and paying it forward. The story included an interview with Shirley Brooks-Jones, who happened to be a passenger on Delta Flight 15 flying from Frankfurt, Germany, to Atlanta, Georgia. And here's the story she told.[6]

On September 11, 2001, when American airspace was suddenly shut down, thirty-eight jumbo jets blocked from their US destinations landed in Gander, Newfoundland. Eight thousand passengers got off those jets in Gander, an area whose population is just ten thousand. As those thousands of passengers sat on the tarmac at the airport, the leaders from the very small surrounding towns were putting their heads together. The pastors, the mayors, the Salvation Army coordinators all asked themselves: *What are we going to do with all the Plane People?* They called them by this name.

Each tiny town stepped forth bravely to accept X number of passengers and welcomed the Plane People like lost brothers and sisters. They closed down the businesses. They closed down the schools. Old people, young people, little children—all came running with sheets, pillows, blankets, towels, and washcloths from their own homes. Their sole focus became caring for the Plane People, who were so far away from their homes and the people they loved. Satellite TV was installed in every service club and church and school where the guests were staying so that each stranded passenger could know what was happening in the United States. Banks of phones were set up so that all the guests could call home as often as they wished, at no charge. The Plane People were treated tenderly and compassionately by these small-town Newfoundlanders who could least afford it.

After three days, American airspace opened back up, and the Plane People could return home. But by that time, it was actually difficult for them to leave. The men, the women, and the children were all crying because they didn't want to be parted from those big-hearted Newfoundlanders who had saved them and had done so much for them. The passengers tried to leave money to pay for the assistance they had received, but none of it was accepted.

On Flight 15 returning to Atlanta, a physician on board said he had learned during his stay that many of the students in the small towns were dropping out of school because there were no jobs. So, Shirley Brooks-Jones, the passenger later interviewed for the NPR segment, said, "Why don't we start a scholarship fund?" She immediately made up pledge sheets, and the plane's captain enthusiastically made the first pledge. When Shirley collected the sheets from fellow passengers, she discovered that they had pledged over $15,000. Today, the fund, over a million dollars, has altered the future for many of the young people in and around Gander. Two hundred twenty-eight young people have received Flight 15 scholarships. Three or four of them are now medical doctors, and a number of them have gone on for master's degrees and PhDs.

The passengers of Flight 15 honored the Newfound-landers' lavish and random acts of kindness and paid it forward, making a future possible for these remote communities.

When you consider your own life's pay-it-forward stories, what random acts of kindness have you received? How have you sought to pay it forward?

Glimpse the holy right where you are

Thirty-six years ago my husband and I moved to Milwaukee from a small, trendy university community filled with art, political rallies, and progressive thinkers. The first couple of weeks after we moved here, I would stand at the kitchen sink, look out the window, and cry. My secret prayer was "Dear God, do not let me live and die in Milwaukee." Now, after more than three decades in this city, I'm not moving anytime soon! Buddhist monk and author Thich Nhat Hanh says, "This spot where you sit is your own spot. It is on this very spot and in this very moment that you can become enlightened. You don't have to sit beneath a special tree in a distant land."[7] I've grown to value the art, political rallies, and progressive thinkers *here—in Milwaukee.* I look forward to functions at the colleges and universities *here*. For decades now, our family has been a part of one faith community *here*. And I'm deeply attached to Milwaukee's gorgeous lakefront with its harbor walk, fishing piers, and lighthouses. In my backyard there are deer, wild turkeys, and an occasional fox, yet I can be in the center of the city for music or theater in fifteen minutes. And there's more to appreciate: I've made friends in Milwaukee, many cherished friends who have transformed my life.

The ancient idea of pilgrimage invites us to consider a sacred journey to a holy place, traditionally a place like Medjugorje or Mecca or Rome. But I'm not all that sure we have to go far at all. Thich Nhat Hanh says, "The path around our home is also the ground of awakening."[8] Curiously enough, Milwaukee has become my ground of awakening.

The practice of finding nudges us to consider the holy right where we are: in our home or in our backyard or in our town, showing us the value in the place where we live and teaching us to actively seek out the holy.

Dayenu is a Hebrew word meaning "It would have been enough for us." A significant part of every Jewish Seder, the *Dayenu* lets us glimpse the holy as it expresses thanks for God's blessings. Here's an excerpt:

Had You fed us manna,
but not given us the Shabbat,

it would have been enough for us!
Had You given us the Shabbat,
but not brought us to Mount Sinai,
it would have been enough for us!
Had You given us the Torah,
but not brought us into the Land of Israel,
it would have been enough for us![9]

Practicing *dayenu* teaches us the joy of the journey, the embrace of the process, the satisfaction of each individual step. *Dayenu* is a profound practice of finding because it doesn't require fulfillment or getting to the end but lifts up all the thanksgivings along the way. *Dayenu* is an affirmation of faith that proclaims that the God of deliverance is with us on the journey and that each single step is enough. Rabbi Irwin Kula writes,

> If we were to practice *dayenu* every morning and every night before we went to sleep, imagine how we'd reframe our goals and anxieties; how differently we'd parse our day. "If I walk into my kids' room just before they awaken and see them stir, and nothing else happens today, *dayenu*. If I have breakfast with them, but I fail to close the deal this afternoon, *dayenu*. If I close the deal but miss a date with an old friend, *dayenu*." *Dayenu* is like a marinade for our

consciousness. The more time we dwell there, the richer and more delicious life becomes.[10]

In your practice of finding, begin by thanking God for each step along the way. One way to explore those steps is by writing your own *dayenu*.

When we value what we have and are no longer frantically seeking, we enter into a profound contentment of enough. We practice finding David Steindl-Rast's "great fullness" as we savor the abundance around us.

Practices and Ponderings

A First Spiritual Exercise:
List Everything That Love Provides in Your Life

This suggestion from author Christina Baldwin[11] has pulled me back to gratitude many, many times. Even on the bleakest of days, there is lots of grist here for the practice of finding.

The other day I was going through that drawer of cherished cards and letters I've kept over many decades. A number of them are from our daughter, Katie. She ends almost every one with "Aren't we lucky?" This enduring refrain has inspired me time and time again. She's referring to relationship, to the power of connection, to the enduring bond of love. It's always been awful to say good-bye to her, whether she was leaving for India for her sophomore year of high school, or going to college in Ohio, or traveling to London for work. But she has said at every parting, "Aren't we lucky?," which means: *Aren't we grateful we love each other this much?*

Make a list of everything you can think of that love provides in your life and offer abundant thanks.

A Second Spiritual Exercise: Remember Your Books

My needs are met when I have good books! Dr. Seuss reminds us, "The more that you read, the more things you will know. The more that you learn, the more places you'll go."[12] I am unceasingly thankful for my ability to read and for my books—the books I possess and the books I own in my heart and mind. My mother was a librarian, and her lifelong gift was raising our family with lots of books. Books take us on fantastic adventures as we visit places we see only in our imaginations. They teach us courage as we read memoirs or biographies of heroes through the ages. Remember the books you couldn't put down and the books that have shaped the You that you are today.

A Third Spiritual Exercise:
Meditate on a Contentment Mantra

"Contentment is an inexhaustible treasure," says an Arabic proverb.[13] Briefly meditate upon this proverb morning and evening for a week. Reflect on how the repetition of this mantra is deepening your practice of finding.

Questions to Ponder

Reflect on happiness that money can't buy

- What are your top three joys that money can't buy?
- What free-of-charge pleasures bring you the contentment of enough?

Be glad when your needs are met

- Reread the stanza from Lao Tzu: "Be content with what you have; / rejoice in the way things are. / When you realize there is nothing lacking, / the whole world belongs to you."[14] How do these words help you to be glad when your needs are met? How do these words help you to practice finding?
- As you look back on very stressful chapters of your life, what basic needs were still being met during

these times? What was in place that brought you the contentment of enough? How did you practice finding?

Glimpse the holy right where you are

- ❧ What holiness is right in front of you?
- ❧ How does glimpsing the holy right where you are help you to find the contentment of enough?
- ❧ Where is God in this?

Acknowledgments

Thank you . . .

Anne McMahon Hesse, wordsmith, manuscript reader, and faithful friend—whose perspective and articulateness rescued me time and time again. There are not enough words of thanks for Anne.

Mary Hietbrink, editor at Eerdmans, who brought everything together with insight and grace.

Wayne Muller, author, for his kindness in writing the foreword.

Chris Glaser, author.

Kathleen Adams, longtime friend.

Kind and generous reference librarians at the Elm Grove Public Library: Noah Weckwerth, Sue Daniels, Lori Kuban, Abby Landers, Paulette Brooks, and library director Sarah Muench.

Members of the Wisconsin Go Hiking Club, who keep me fit and sane.

Beloved "Monday Sisters": Donna, Marty, Nancy, Claire, and Elaine.

Jim and Jill Ardis and the gang at the Gathering, who help me see a larger world.

All of my retreatants and spiritual direction seekers, who teach me by sharing their paths to faith and wisdom.

My dear family: John, David and Laura, Katie and Dan, and John David, whose love sustains me.

How to Use This Book with a Group

As you prepare to lead this book study, take notes on what seems particularly interesting or conducive to discussion. Reflect upon how you want to present the material. Be sure to make use of the "Practices and Ponderings" at the end of each chapter. And ask yourself these questions:

- What topics or practices or questions call for solitude and reflection?
- What topics or practices or questions might be useful for individual journaling?
- What topics or practices or questions would be best suited to large group or small group discussion?

Here are some suggestions to make your group experience as enriching as possible.

For a four-week book study, study two chapters each week. Each session should be 1½ hours to 2 hours in length. Work with one chapter at a time and take a short break between chapters.

For an eight-week book study, study one chapter each week. These sessions should be 45 minutes to one hour in length.

For the first session:

- Provide a kind and generous welcome.
- Make sure that participants are introduced to each other. You may want to use nametags.
- Explain the importance of the book study, either by expressing it in your own words or by reading the back cover. Introduce the practice of finding as a spiritual opportunity.
- Ask the participants to utilize the "End the Day with Thanks" inventory (page 72) each night: *What have been my sources of grace this day? For what do I give thanks?* In subsequent meetings, check in with the participants and ask them how that daily inventory is going. What are they learning about themselves and thankfulness?

For subsequent sessions:

- As you begin each week, remind the participants of this Whitcomb quotation: "When we engage in finding, we recognize with humility and wonder

that the universe contains possibilities beyond our power to imagine."
· Begin the discussion of each chapter by asking members of the group what caught their attention.
· Continue to share thoughts and ideas. Vary the meeting framework from week to week so there's a variety of quiet time, individual journaling, and large or small group sharing.
· As you move toward adjournment each week, remind the participants when the next session will be and what chapter(s) they should read in preparation.
· You can end each session with your own prayer, or you may wish to use a short prayer like this one:

Loving Spirit, we thank you for the gift of gratitude
which sustains us in good times and in bad.
Help us to practice finding each day
so that we may pay attention
to all that enriches us and
all that is gracious and lovely. Amen.

For the last session, ask the participants these questions before the closing prayer:

What will you remember most from this book study?
How can you continue to practice finding each day?

The Practice of Finding Retreat: Leader's Guide

Planning Ahead

This retreat format is ideal for *one day* but can be used for a day and a half or two days if more free time is built in or if longer times for reflection are added. Review the material below and get comfortable with all the parts of the retreat. You may choose to use a combination of handouts, newsprint, PowerPoint, or other means to share information. Someone on the planning team should be familiar with the physical layout of the retreat location and be able to talk about logistics. Place chairs in a circle if the number of retreat participants allows that. Create sacred space by placing a small, low altar table in the middle of the circle. If you wish, cover the table with a cloth, plants, flowers, or other appropriate symbols. Next, light a candle and take some time to pray for yourself and for those who will attend the retreat. Then relax, look forward to the day, and enjoy the retreat yourself.

Morning

Introduction

Say: The practice of finding often takes our breath away and brings tears to our eyes, for through these precious and unforeseen "aha" moments we discover that the gift we receive is more cherished than the one we've been seeking. When we engage in finding, we recognize with humility and wonder that the universe contains possibilities beyond our power to imagine.

Welcome and Greetings

Welcome participants, review the outline of the day, thank any particular planners or meal preparers, and share the location of bathrooms, the dining room, and the breakout space.

Opening Song

Have participants sing "Morning Has Broken," all verses, or another song of your choosing. Singing can be done with accompaniment or a cappella. Ask those who are able to stand to do so.

Opening Prayer

Say: Generous and abundant God, we thank you that we are gathered today to learn about the practice of finding. We thank you for all of your mercies, your grace, and your deep love for us. Open our hearts to receive and to share. May your Spirit guide and bless each one of us, we pray. Amen.

Opening Exercise

Say: Learning to savor is an integral part of the practice of finding. Think about your five senses and what they have recently absorbed and relished. Using the blank space on one of your handouts, finish this sentence: *During this past week, I remember savoring* _____.

As we go around the circle, please share
- your name
- your sentence about savoring (if you're comfortable sharing it)

Morning Practices Facilitated by the Large-Group Leader

Listening to an excerpt from the diary of Samuel Lane (see page 9)

Say: Born in 1718, Samuel Lane of Stratham, New Hampshire, was a farmer, surveyor, shoemaker, and tanner who kept a journal for sixty-five years. On Thanksgiving Day, November 21, 1793, he rose before daylight and recorded his "Many Mercies." I will read this slowly so you can catch every word and reflect on this charming diary entry.

Ask: As you listened to this, what did you notice? What attracted your attention? How might you be guided by Samuel Lane to appreciate simple pleasures?

Ask: Author Holly Whitcomb notes that she has shared this diary reading at her Thanksgiving table. Is this something you might want to use with your friends or family?

Listing Sources of Abundance

Give participants a few minutes to list their sources of abundance. Encourage them to put down anything that comes to mind. Then ask them, "Did anything on your list surprise you?" Discuss. Next, ask them, "How many of the items on your list cost money?" Discuss.

Sharing Answered Prayers

Say: We often talk about unanswered prayers, but answered prayers manifest themselves in dozens of different ways and are an effective way to practice finding. Have you experienced *healing* or *assistance* or *resolution* or *clarity* or *reconciliation*? [Repeat this last sentence.] Think about this for a little while. Then take a few minutes to list on a blank sheet your answered prayers from this date last year to this date this year. [Pause.] Does anyone feel comfortable sharing aloud any of their answered prayers? [If no one volunteers, move on.]

Spending Time in Silent Reflection

Say: Empty your lap of books or papers and begin by sitting quietly with your eyes closed. In the quiet of your soul, name the person who most believed in you as a child, and silently give thanks for that person's love and encouragement. [Wait several minutes.] Please continue to keep your eyes closed for another exercise. I want you to think about your whole day yesterday. Think about your morning and where you were and what you were doing. Spend some time thinking about the middle of the day. Reflect on your evening and your going to bed, where you were and what you were doing. Now, as you think about the whole day yesterday, ask yourself two questions to be held in your heart: What were your sources of grace? And for what do you give thanks? [Take a long pause. After a minute or two, ask participants to slowly open their eyes.] Author Holly Whitcomb shares that she asks herself these two questions every night before she falls asleep. Would this be a good practice-of-finding inventory for you?

*Reflecting upon the Importance of
Not Wasting Your Suffering*

Say: Wendell Berry, a Kentucky farmer, is one of our greatest living American poets. Like Jesus, he often relies on agricultural images as metaphors in his teaching. In his poem "The Sycamore," he writes eloquently of the resilience of an old, scarred sycamore tree. We're going to study this poem together by a method called *Lectio Divina* or "Divine Reading." This method is usually used to study Scripture, but it can also be used with poetry or literature.

Step One: Listen for words or phrases as I read the poem aloud. [Read the poem on page 53.]

Reading of Poem

Ask: What words or phrases caught your attention?

Step Two: Listen for themes or ideas as [name of volunteer] reads the poem aloud. [Pass the book to the volunteer.]

Reading of Poem

Ask: What themes or ideas emerged this time?

Step Three: Listen for God's invitation through the poem or what God might be asking of you as [name of second volunteer] reads the poem aloud. [Pass the book to the volunteer.]

Reading of Poem

Ask: What is God asking of you through this poem? What is God's invitation?

Time Apart (30 minutes)

Hand out a sheet with the following exercises and questions for participants to reflect upon in solitude and remind them what time to come back. (You may also want to remind them where the bathrooms are and where they can get coffee.) Physical space may allow participants to sit quietly in the meeting room or go to various breakout rooms.

1. Reflect upon Wendell Berry's poem "The Sycamore."

- In what ways are you like this sycamore?
- What wounds have you received?
- What wounds have you redeemed?

2. Create a stream-of-consciousness list called "What Suffering Has Taught Me." Take some time here. How have you made use of and not wasted your suffering? What have you learned?

Small-Group Discussion (20 minutes)

Regroup by singing verses one, two, and four of the hymn "For the Beauty of the Earth," or sing another hymn of your choosing (with accompaniment or a cappella). Break the large group into small groups of three to five people by asking them to cluster their chairs together or to count off in some way and then move to their group. Have these groups discuss whatever they feel comfortable sharing from the solitude time.

Lunch Break

(1 to 1½ hours depending on whether there is opportunity to go outside after lunch). A lunch blessing may be prayed or sung.

Afternoon

Sing a gathering song. Singing can be done with accompaniment or a cappella. Ask those who are able to stand to do so. Choose one of these hymns or another song of your choice:

- "Now Thank We All Our God" (traditional Thanksgiving hymn), perhaps verses one and three
- "Count Your Blessings" (old gospel hymn), perhaps verses one and four

Opening Exercise

Say: Who you are and how you maintain perspective may be shaped by favorite sayings or quotations. What are some of your family's sayings or your favorite quotations? Who feels comfortable sharing?

Reflecting upon a Random Act of Kindness

Say: I will read the following story, which talks about a random act of kindness and paying it forward. [See the story of Gander on pages 134–36.]

    Ask: What random acts of kindness have you received? How have you paid it forward? Who wants to begin?

Time Apart: The Practice of Finding Yourself (30 minutes)

Hand out a sheet with the following exercises for participants to reflect upon in solitude, and remind them what time to come back together. Physical space may allow them to sit quietly in the meeting room or to go to various breakout rooms.

Draw your essence. Go over to the art supply table and get some blank paper, some markers, some colored pencils, or whatever materials you wish. Think of a metaphor that represents your essence, then make a simple drawing.

Compose a prayer of thanksgiving about yourself. The practice of finding compels us to reflect with awe on the many and astounding aspects of ourselves. Each of us is one of a kind. After considering your uniqueness, compose a prayer of thanksgiving about yourself. If you wish, illustrate your prayer with any of the art supplies.

Say (after 30 minutes): You have spent some time thinking about your essence and composing a prayer of thanksgiving about yourself. Any comments on that process? How did it feel? Let's talk together.

Considering Busyness: A Hindrance to Gratitude

Say: We are all occasionally crushed by an insidious busyness that dries up our souls and definitely hinders the practice of finding. At these times, we are withered, weary, and overcome. In our overwhelmedness, thankfulness is nowhere to be found. Listen to these wise words, "How Many Eggs Can You Hold?," from Wayne Muller. [Read the piece on pages 123-24.]

Small-Group Discussion (20 minutes)

Break the large group into small groups of three to five people, perhaps the same small groups as those in the morning. Have them discuss the following questions, which can be dictated or put on PowerPoint or newsprint.

- What do you make of this reading?
- How is busyness a hindrance to your gratitude?
- How many "eggs" can you hold?
- Right now, is there anything you need to put down?

Closing Ritual Facilitated by
the Large-Group Leader

Bring the large group back together and ask them what they will most remember from this practice-of-finding retreat. Discuss briefly.

Say: Please join me in our unison commission. These are the words from Holly Whitcomb with which we began our day:

> The practice of finding often takes our breath away and brings tears to our eyes, for through these precious and unforeseen "aha" moments we discover that the gift we receive is more cherished than the one we've been seeking. When we engage in finding, we recognize with humility and wonder that the universe contains possibilities beyond our power to imagine.

Then ask the group to join you in a closing song such as "Amazing Grace," verse four (a good verse of finding):

> Through many dangers, toils, and snares,
> I have already come;
> 'Tis grace has brought me safe thus far,
> and grace will lead me home.

Notes

Introduction

1. Barbara Brown Taylor, *Leaving Church: A Memoir of Faith* (New York: HarperSanFrancisco, 2006), 225.

Chapter One

1. Sonya Lyubomirsky, "Eight Steps toward a More Satisfying Life," *Time*, January 17, 2005, A8.

2. Quoted in Esther de Waal, *Lost in Wonder: Rediscovering the Spiritual Art of Attentiveness* (Collegeville, MN: Liturgical Press, 2003), 72.

3. Thornton Wilder, *Our Town: A Play in Three Acts* (New York: Scholastic, 1957), 100.

4. Quoted in Carl Franz and Lorena Havens, *The People's Guide to Mexico* (Emeryville, CA: Avalon Travel, 2006), 212.

5. Samuel Lane, *A Journal for the Years 1739–1803*, ed. Charles Lane Hanson (Concord, NH: New Hampshire Historical Society, 1937), 21–22.

6. Thich Nhat Hanh, *Living Buddha, Living Christ* (New York: Riverhead Books, 1995), 14.

7. Sheila Weller, *Girls like Us: Carole King, Joni Mitchell, Carly Simon—and the Journey of a Generation* (New York: Atria Books, 2008), 353–54.

8. Sonya Lyubomirsky, *The Myths of Happiness: What Should Make You Happy but Doesn't, What Shouldn't Make You Happy, but Does* (New York: Penguin, 2013), 178.

9. Anne Lamott, *Help, Thanks, Wow: The Three Essential Prayers* (New York: Riverhead Books, 2012), 81.

10. Idea from Nelle Morton, *The Journey Is Home* (Boston: Beacon, 1985), 127–28.

11. Mary Pipher, *Seeking Peace: Chronicles of the Worst Buddhist in the World* (New York: Riverhead Books, 2009), 243.

Chapter Two

1. Quoted in James Baraz and Shoshana Alexander, *Awakening Joy: 10 Steps That Will Put You on the Road to Real Happiness* (New York: Bantam Books, 2010), 67.

2. Melissa Tidwell, "Editor's Note," *Alive Now*, November/December 2003, 2.

3. Sara Miles, *Take This Bread: A Radical Conversion* (New York: Ballantine Books, 2007), 222.

4. Anne Lamott, *Grace (Eventually): Thoughts on Faith* (New York: Riverhead Books, 2007), 129.

5. Philip Simmons, *Learning to Fall: The Blessings of an Imperfect Life* (New York: Bantam Books, 2003), 37.

6. Philippa Perry, *How to Stay Sane* (New York: Picador, 2012), 88–90.

7. Quoted in Maggie Oman Shannon, *The Way We Pray: Prayer Practices from Around the World* (Berkeley, CA: Conari, 2001), 76.

8. Thich Nhat Hanh, *The Long Road Turns to Joy: A Guide to Walking Meditation* (Berkeley, CA: Parallax, 1996), 36.

Chapter Three

1. Quoted in Elizabeth Gilbert, *Big Magic: Creative Living Beyond Fear* (New York: Riverhead Books, 2015), 247.

2. Richard Rohr, *Falling Upward: A Spirituality for the Two Halves of Life* (San Francisco: Jossey-Bass, 2011), xx.

3. Mary Pipher, *Seeking Peace: Chronicles of the Worst Buddhist in the World* (New York: Riverhead Books, 2009), 172.

4. Mark Nepo, *Seven Thousand Ways to Listen: Staying Close to What Is Sacred* (New York: Free Press, 2012), 47.

5. Friedrich Nietszche, *Twilight of the Idols and The Anti-Christ*, trans. Michael Tanner (New York: Penguin, 1990), 33.

6. Taken from Conan O'Brien's commencement speech at Dartmouth College, Hanover, New Hampshire, June 12, 2011.

7. Barbara Brown Taylor, *An Altar in the World: A Geography of Faith* (New York: HarperOne, 2009), 72–73.

8. Robert McAfee Brown, ed., *The Essential Reinhold Niebuhr: Selected Essays and Addresses* (New Haven, CT: Yale University Press, 1986), 251.

9. Quoted in Anne Lamott, *Hallelujah Anyway: Rediscovering Mercy* (New York: Riverhead Books, 2017), 136.

10. Idea from John R. Claypool, *The Hopeful Heart* (Harrisburg, PA: Morehouse, 2003), 23.

11. Elizabeth Lesser, *Broken Open: How Difficult Times Can Help Us Grow* (New York: Villard Books, 2005), 243–44.

12. Anne Lamott, *Help, Thanks, Wow: The Three Essential Prayers* (New York: Riverhead Books, 2012), 50.

13. Ideas from Julius Segal, "Life Crisis! The Five Techniques You Need to Survive," *Parents*, July 1986, 63–67.

14. Wendell Berry, *Collected Poems, 1957–1982* (New York: North Point, 1996), 65.

15. Rosamund Stone Zander and Benjamin Zander, *The Art of Possibility* (New York: Penguin Books, 2000), 31.

16. Etty Hillesum, *An Interrupted Life and Letters from Westerbork* (New York: Henry Holt, 1996), 327.

17. Robert Yoder, "Afraid of What Might Follow," *These Days* (July–September 2015): daily reading for September 18.

Chapter Four

1. Quoted in Lauren F. Winner, *Wearing God: Clothing, Laughter, Fire, and Other Overlooked Ways of Meeting God* (New York: HarperOne, 2015), 17–18.

2. Quoted in Esther de Waal, *Lost in Wonder: Rediscovering the Spiritual Art of Attentiveness* (Collegeville, MN: Liturgical Press, 2003), 21.

3. Based on the story from these two sources: "Passenger Lands Plane after Pilot Is Stricken," *The Milwaukee Journal*, February 21, 1987, and Jan Tucker, "Man Has Crash Course in Flying," *The Daily Globe*, February 21, 1987.

4. Barbara Brown Taylor, *An Altar in the World: A Geography of Faith* (New York: HarperOne, 2009), 184–85.

5. Ram Dass, *Still Here: Embracing Aging, Changing, and Dying* (New York: Riverhead Books, 2001), 4, 201.

6. Dass, *Still Here*, 200–201.

7. Daniel Ladinsky, trans., *Love Poems from God:*

Twelve Sacred Voices from the East and West (New York: Penguin, 2002), 52.

8. Atul Gawande, *Being Mortal: Medicine and What Matters in the End* (New York: Metropolitan Books, 2014), 238–39.

9. Anthony De Mello, *Sadhana, a Way to God: Christian Exercises in Eastern Form* (New York: Image Books, 1984), 140.

10. Jonathan Rosenbaum, *Discovering Orson Welles* (Berkeley, CA: University of California Press, 2007), 112.

11. Maya Angelou, *Wouldn't Take Nothing for My Journey Now* (New York: Bantam Books, 1993), 73–74.

12. Quoted in M. J. Ryan, *Attitudes of Gratitude: How to Give and Receive Joy Every Day of Your Life* (Berkeley, CA: Conari, 1999), 63–64.

13. Alexander Carmichael, *Carmina Gadelica: Hymns and Cantations*, vol. 3 (Edinburgh: Oliver and Boyd, 1940), 59.

14. Joyce Rupp, *The Cup of Life: A Guide to Spiritual Growth* (Notre Dame, IN: Ave Maria, 1997), 150.

15. Mirabai Starr, trans., *The Showings of Julian of Norwich: A New Translation* (Charlottesville, VA: Hampton Roads, 2013), 67.

Chapter Five

1. Barbara Brown Taylor, *An Altar in the World: A Geography of Faith* (New York: HarperOne, 2009), 206.

2. Mark 1:11, quoted from *The New Testament and Psalms: An Inclusive Version*, ed. Victor Roland Gold et al. (New York: Oxford University Press, 1995), 54–55.

3. Henri J. M. Nouwen, *The Only Necessary Thing*, ed. Wendy Wilson Greer (New York: Crossroad, 1999), 67.

4. Gordan Peerman, *Blessed Relief: What Christians Can Learn from Buddhists about Suffering* (Woodstock, VT: Skylight Paths, 2008), 47.

5. Manfred F. R. Kets de Vries, *The Hedgehog Effect* (San Francisco: Jossey-Bass, 2011), 138.

6. Rachel Naomi Remen, *My Grandfather's Blessings: Stories of Strength, Refuge, and Belonging* (New York: Riverhead Books, 2000), 27.

7. Jack Kornfield, *No Time like the Present: Finding Freedom, Love, and Joy Right Where You Are* (New York: Atria Books, 2017), 143–44.

8. Idea from Marva J. Dawn, *Being Well While We're Ill: Wholeness and Hope in Spite of Infirmity* (Minneapolis: Augsburg, 2008), 172 73.

9. Wayne Muller, *Learning to Pray: How We Find Heaven on Earth* (New York: Bantam Books, 2003), 104.

10. Norman Cousins, *Anatomy of An Illness as Perceived*

by the Patient: Reflections on Healing and Regeneration (New York: W.W. Norton, 1979), 72–73.

11. Christina Baldwin, *Life's Companion: Journal Writing as a Spiritual Quest* (New York: Bantam Books, 1991), 232.

12. Emily Dickinson, *The Complete Poems of Emily Dickinson*, ed. Thomas H. Johnson (Boston: Little, Brown and Company, 1960), 706.

Chapter Six

1. Marianne Williamson, *A Return to Love: Reflections on the Principles of a Course in Miracles* (New York: Harper Perennial, 1993), 191.

2. Madeleine L'Engle, *Anytime Prayers* (Wheaton, IL: Harold Shaw, 1994), 52.

3. Jalal al-Din Rumi, *Feeling the Shoulder of the Lion: Poetry and Teaching Stories of Rumi*, trans. Coleman Barks (Boston: Shambhala, 1991), 9.

4. Idea from Nina Lesowitz and Mary Beth Sammons, *Living Life as a Thank You: The Transformative Power of Daily Gratitude* (San Francisco: Viva Editions, 2009), 51–52.

5. This is the link to the NPR transcript from which my version of the story is taken: http://www.npr.org/sections/goatsandsoda/2017/02/09/513700808/while-others-saw refugees-this-german-professor-saw-human-potential.

6. Toinette Lippe, *Nothing Left Over: A Plain and Simple Life* (New York: Jeremy P. Tarcher, 2002), 128.

7. Quoted in Sharon Salzberg, *Real Love: The Art of Mindful Connection* (New York: Flatiron Books, 2017), 159.

8. Mark Nepo, *The Book of Awakening: Having the Life You Want by Being Present to the Life You Have* (Berkeley, CA: Conari, 2000), 226.

9. This quotation is widely attributed to Oscar Wilde. It is also the title of a book by Mike Robbins, published by Jossey-Bass in 2009.

10. Jack Kornfield, *A Path with Heart: A Guide through the Perils and Promises of Spiritual Life* (New York: Bantam Books, 1993), 81.

11. Lillian Daniel and Martin B. Copenhaver, *This Odd and Wondrous Calling: The Public and Private Lives of Two Ministers* (Grand Rapids: Eerdmans, 2009), 109.

12. *The Random House Dictionary of the English Language*, 2nd ed., unabridged, ed. Stuart Berg Flexner (New York: Random House, 1987), s.v. "essence."

13. Dawna Markova, *I Will Not Die an Unlived Life: Proclaiming Purpose and Passion* (Berkeley, CA: Conari, 2000), 75.

14. Eleanor Roosevelt, *You Learn by Living* (New York: Harper and Brothers, 1960), 29–30.

15. Harriet Lerner, *The Dance of Fear: Rising above Anxiety, Fear, and Shame to Be Your Best and Bravest Self* (New York: Perennial Currents, 2005), 210–11.

16. Anaïs Nin, *The Diary of Anaïs Nin*, vol. 3: *1939–1944*, ed. Gunther Stuhlmann (New York: Harcourt Brace Jovanovich, 1969), 125.

17. Marjory Zoet Bankson, *Creative Aging: Rethinking Retirement and Non-Retirement in a Changing World* (Woodstock, VT: Skylight Paths, 2010), 17.

18. Sheryl Sandberg and Adam Grant, *Option B: Facing Adversity, Building Resilience, and Finding Joy* (New York: Knopf, 2017), 68.

Chapter Seven

1. Holly W. Whitcomb, *Seven Spiritual Gifts of Waiting* (Minneapolis: Augsburg, 2005), 67.

2. Anne Morrow Lindbergh, *Gift from the Sea* (New York: Vintage Books, 1955), 114.

3. James Baraz and Shoshana Alexander, *Awakening Joy: 10 Steps That Will Put You on the Road to Real Happiness* (New York: Bantam Books, 2010), 160.

4. Quoted in Baraz and Alexander, *Awakening Joy*, 158.

5. Quoted in Greg McKeown, *Essentialism: The Disciplined Pursuit of Less* (New York: Crown Business, 2014), 225.

6. Quoted in Taylor, *Leaving Church*, 230.

7. Wayne Muller, *Learning to Pray: How We Find Heaven on Earth* (New York: Bantam Books, 2003), 141.

8. Robert McAfee Brown, ed., *The Essential Reinhold Niebuhr: Selected Essays and Addresses* (New Haven, CT: Yale University Press, 1986), 251.

9. Quoted in Baraz and Alexander, *Awakening Joy*, 101.

10. Kathleen Fischer, *Autumn Gospel: Women in the Second Half of Life* (Mahwah, NJ: Integration Books, 1995), 17.

11. Wayne Muller, *A Life of Being, Having, and Doing Enough* (New York: Harmony Books, 2010), 153.

12. Hafiz, "Your Mother and My Mother," in *The Gift: Poems by Hafiz, the Great Sufi Master*, trans. Daniel Ladinsky (New York: Penguin, 1999), 39.

Chapter Eight

1. Sue Monk Kidd, *Firstlight: The Early Inspirational Writings of Sue Monk Kidd* (New York: Guideposts Books, 2006), 124–25.

2. Quoted in Maggie Oman Shannon, *The Way We Pray: Prayer Practices from Around the World* (Berkeley, CA: Conari, 2001), 40.

3. Anthony De Mello, *The Song of the Bird* (New York: Image Books, 1984), 131.

4. Lao Tzu, *Tao Te Ching: A New English Version*, trans. Stephen Mitchell (New York: Harper Perennial, 1988), 44.

5. William Sloane Coffin, *Letters to a Young Doubter* (Louisville: Westminster John Knox, 2005), 78.

6. This is the link to the NPR transcript from which my version of the story is taken: http://www.npr.org /2016/09/10/493399783/in-wake-of-international-tragedy rerouted-passengers-find-resilience-in-gander-o.

7. Thich Nhat Hanh, *The Miracle of Mindfulness: An Introduction to the Practice of Meditation*, trans. Mobi Ho (Boston: Beacon, 1975), 57.

8. Thich Nhat Hanh, *Present Moment, Wonderful Moment: Mindfulness Verses for Daily Living* (Berkeley, CA: Parallax, 1990), 39.

9. *The Shalom Seders: Three Haggadahs*, ed. New Jewish Agenda (New York: Adama Books, 1984), 25.

10. Irwin Kula with Linda Loewenthal, *Yearnings: Embracing the Sacred Messiness of Life* (New York: Hyperion, 2006), 255.

11. Christina Baldwin, *Life's Companion: Journal Writing as a Spiritual Quest* (New York: Bantam Books, 1991), 188.

12. Dr. Seuss, *I Can Read with My Eyes Shut!* (New York: Random House, 1978), 27.

13. Al-Qushayri, *The Principles of Sufism*, trans. B. R. von Schlegell (Oneonta, NY: Mizan, 1992), 109.

14. Lao Tzu, *Tao Te Ching: A New English Version*, trans. Stephen Mitchell (New York: Harper Perennial, 1988), 44.

Selected Bibliography

Baraz, James, and Shoshana Alexander. *Awakening Joy: 10 Steps That Will Put You on the Road to Real Happiness.* New York: Bantam Books, 2010.

Barks, Coleman, trans. *Feeling the Shoulder of the Lion: Poetry and Teaching Stories of Rumi.* Boston: Shambhala, 1991.

Berry, Wendell. *Collected Poems: 1957–1982.* New York: North Point Press, 1996.

Brown, Brené. *The Gifts of Imperfection: Let Go of Who You Think You're Supposed to Be and Embrace Who You Are.* Center City, MN: Hazelden, 2010.

Carmichael, Alexander. *Carmina Gadelica: Hymns and Incantations.* Vol. 3. Edinburgh: Oliver and Boyd, 1940.

Chittister, Joan D. *Scarred by Struggle, Transformed by Hope.* Grand Rapids: Eerdmans, 2003.

Coffin, William Sloane. *Letters to a Young Doubter.* Louisville: Westminster John Knox, 2005.

Daniel, Lillian, and Martin B. Copenhaver. *This Odd and

Wondrous Calling: The Public and Private Lives of Two Ministers. Grand Rapids: Eerdmans, 2009.

Dass, Ram. *Still Here: Embracing Aging, Changing, and Dying.* New York: Riverhead Books, 2001.

De Mello, Anthony, S.J. *Sadhana: A Way to God: Christian Exercises in Eastern Form.* New York: Image Books, 1984.

——. *The Song of the Bird.* New York: Image Books, 1984.

De Waal, Esther. *Lost in Wonder: Rediscovering the Spiritual Art of Attentiveness.* Collegeville, MN: Liturgical Press, 2003.

Dickinson, Emily. *The Complete Poems of Emily Dickinson.* Ed. Thomas H. Johnson. Boston: Little, Brown, 1960.

Fritz, Maureena. *Rejoice and Be Glad!* Winona, MN: St. Mary's Press, 1995.

Hagan, Kay Leigh. *Prayers to the Moon: Exercises in Self-Reflection.* San Francisco: HarperSanFrancisco, 1991.

Hillesum, Etty. *An Interrupted Life* and *Letters from Westerbork.* New York: Henry Holt, 1996.

Kornfield, Jack. *No Time like the Present: Finding Freedom, Love, and Joy Right Where You Are.* New York: Atria Books, 2017.

——. *A Path with Heart: A Guide through the Perils and Promises of Spiritual Life.* New York: Bantam Books, 1993.

Ladinsky, Daniel, trans. *The Gift: Poems by Hafiz, the Great Sufi Master.* New York: Penguin, 1999.

—————. *Love Poems from God: Twelve Sacred Voices from the East and West.* New York: Penguin, 2002.

Lamott, Anne. *Grace (Eventually): Thoughts on Faith.* New York: Riverhead Books, 2007.

—————. *Hallelujah Anyway: Rediscovering Mercy.* New York: Riverhead Books, 2017.

—————. *Help, Thanks, Wow: The Three Essential Prayers.* New York: Riverhead Books, 2012.

Lao-Tzu. *Tao Te Ching: A New English Version.* Trans. Stephen Mitchell. New York: Harper Perennial, 1988.

L'Engle, Madeleine. *Anytime Prayers.* Wheaton, IL: Harold Shaw Publishers, 1994.

Lesser, Elizabeth. *Broken Open: How Difficult Times Can Help Us Grow.* New York: Villard Books, 2005.

Lindbergh, Anne Morrow. *Gift from the Sea.* New York: Vintage Books, 1955.

Miles, Sara. *Take This Bread: A Radical Conversion.* New York: Ballantine Books, 2007.

Muller, Wayne. *How, Then, Shall We Live?: Four Simple Questions That Reveal the Beauty and Meaning of Our Lives.* New York: Bantam Books, 1996.

—————. *Learning to Pray: How We Find Heaven on Earth.* New York: Bantam Books, 2003.

—————. *A Life of Being, Having, and Doing Enough.* New York: Harmony Books, 2010.

————. *Sabbath: Restoring the Sacred Rhythm of Rest.* New York: Bantam Books, 1999.

Nepo, Mark. *The Book of Awakening: Having the Life You Want by Being Present to the Life You Have.* Berkeley, CA: Conari, 2000.

Nhat Hanh, Thich. *Living Buddha, Living Christ.* New York: Riverhead Books, 1995.

————. *The Long Road Turns to Joy: A Guide to Walking Meditation.* Berkeley, CA: Parallax, 1996.

————. *The Miracle of Mindfulness: An Introduction to the Practice of Meditation.* Trans. Mobi Ho. Boston: Beacon, 1975.

————. *Present Moment, Wonderful Moment: Mindfulness Verses for Daily Living.* Berkeley, CA: Parallax, 1990.

Nouwen, Henri J. M. *Life of the Beloved: Spiritual Living in a Secular World.* New York: Crossroad, 1992.

————. *The Only Necessary Thing.* Ed. Wendy Wilson Greer. New York: Crossroad, 1999.

Pipher, Mary. *Seeking Peace: Chronicles of the Worst Buddhist in the World.* New York: Riverhead Books, 2009.

Remen, Rachel Naomi. *My Grandfather's Blessings: Stories of Strength, Refuge, and Belonging.* New York: Riverhead Books, 2000.

Rohr, Richard. *Falling Upward: A Spirituality for the Two Halves of Life.* San Francisco: Jossey-Bass, 2011.

Rupp, Joyce. *The Cup of Life: A Guide to Spiritual Growth.* Notre Dame, IN: Ave Maria, 1997.

————. *Open the Door: A Journey to the True Self.* Notre Dame, IN: Sorin Books, 2008.

Sandberg, Sheryl, and Adam Grant. *Option B: Facing Adversity, Building Resilience, and Finding Joy.* New York: Alfred A. Knopf, 2017.

The Shalom Seders: Three Haggadahs. Ed. New Jewish Agenda. New York: Adama Books, 1984.

Taylor, Barbara Brown. *An Altar in the World: A Geography of Faith.* New York: HarperOne, 2009.

————. *Leaving Church: A Memoir of Faith.* New York: HarperSanFrancisco, 2006.

Von Furstenberg, Diane. *The Woman I Wanted to Be.* New York: Simon & Schuster, 2014.

Whitcomb, Holly W. *The Bible and Spiritual Disciplines.* Insights Bible Studies for Growing Faith. Eugene, OR: Wipf and Stock, 2000.

————. *Seven Spiritual Gifts of Waiting.* Minneapolis: Augsburg Fortress, 2005.

Winner, Lauren F. *Wearing God: Clothing, Laughter, Fire, and Other Overlooked Ways of Meeting God.* New York: HarperOne, 2015.

Zander, Rosamund Stone, and Benjamin Zander. *The Art of Possibility.* New York: Penguin, 2000.

About the Author

Holly Wilson Whitcomb has been a pastor and clergy-woman in the United Church of Christ since her graduation from Yale Divinity School and has served churches in Connecticut, Iowa, and Wisconsin. She is also a graduate of the two-year training program for spiritual directors at the Shalem Institute for Spiritual Formation in Washington, DC. As the director of Kettlewood Retreats, Holly travels to churches, retreat houses, and conference centers as she leads retreats and spirituality events around the country. She also spends much of her time as a spiritual director offering one-to-one spiritual direction. She is a jewelry maker and designer who has donated a number of her pieces to charity auctions and who frequently incorporates "art as meditation" into her retreats. Holly is an avid hike leader with a Wisconsin hiking club and loves the outdoors. She plays the classical guitar and is a Threshold Singer who sings to the dying in hospice settings. Holly is the author of dozens of articles on spirituality and the author of four previous books, including *Practicing Your Path* and *Seven Spiritual Gifts of Waiting.* She lives in a suburb of Milwaukee, Wisconsin, with her husband, John. They are the parents of two adult children, David and Kate, and have a grandchild, John David.

You may contact Holly Whitcomb by visiting her website, www.KettlewoodRetreats.com.